Hamlin Avenue

Hamlin Avenue

The time is the 1950s.
The street is Hamlin Avenue, in the small town of
Markham, Illinois, about 25 miles south of Chicago.

Meet the Costello family.

Linda Costello Maurer

Copyright © 2005 by Linda Costello Maurer

All rights reserved. No part of this book may be used or reproduced in any manner whatsoever without written permission of the author.

Printed in the United States of America

ISBN: 1-59571-057-4
Library of Congress Control Number: 2004117577

Word Association Publishers
205 Fifth Avenue
Tarentum, Pennsylvania 15084

This Book is Dedicated to
the loving memory of

Tom & Betty Costello

Acknowledgements

A very special thanks to my brother, Tom Costello. Without his help, encouragement, and guidance, this book would not have been written.

To family and friends who shared their memories and photos, I am very grateful. Many thanks.

A big thank you to my husband, Bob Maurer, for his help in reading and critiquing during the wee hours of the night. Also, thanks for keeping my computer up and running.

Thank you to Doug Ward for his assistance with the cover design.

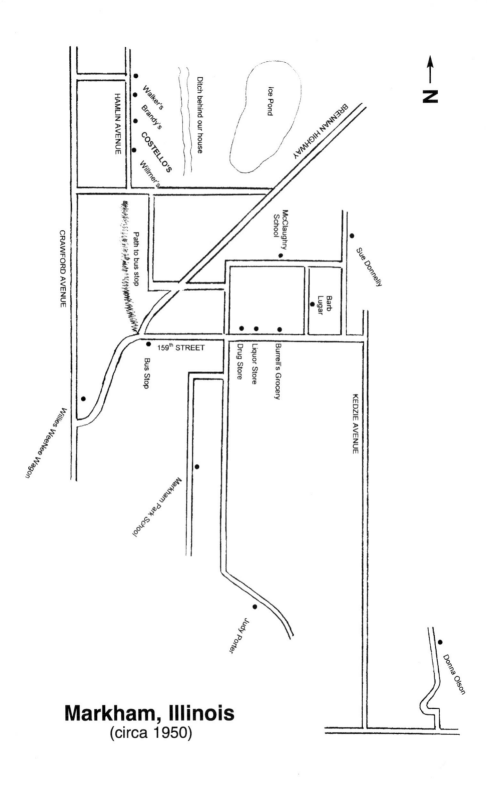

Contents

Prologue: *Riverview Park* • 13

Our Town • 23

Oh, Brother • 31

Father Knows Best • 54

I Remember Mama • 94

It's All Relative • 103

Deck the Halls • 120

A Honey of a Lake • 136

Love Thy Neighbor • 150

Girls Just Want to Have Fun • 156

It's Elementary • 166

Happy Days • 187

2004 - Back to the Future • 201

Poems • 236

GAETANO CASTELLANO FAMILY

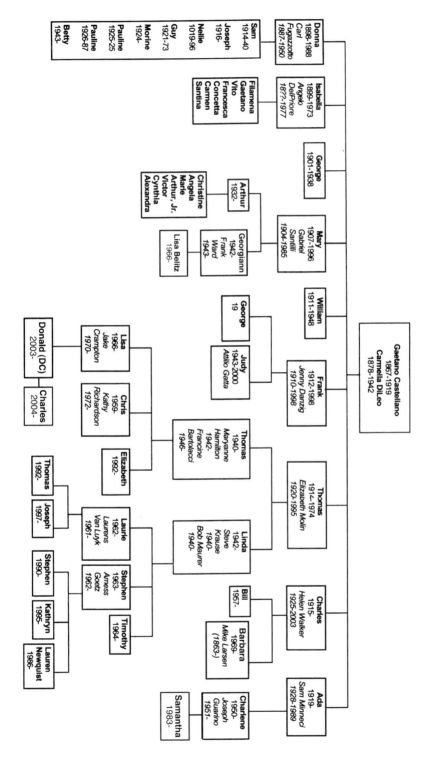

LEONARDO MOLIN FAMILY

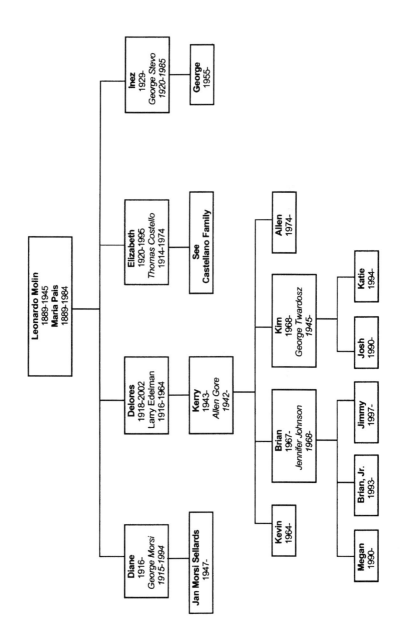

Prologue

August, 1950
Riverview Park
Chicago, Illinois

"Are we almost there yet?" Linda asks. She and Tommy have asked that question every five minutes since they left home. In fact, Tommy, in an effort to be either amusing or irritating, asked it the first time moments after dad had backed out of the driveway onto Hamlin Avenue. They lived 154 blocks south of Chicago's Loop, and Riverview Park was another 32 blocks north, at Belmont and Western. No... they were **not** almost there yet. The anticipation was excruciating — and so was the heat.

"About another 15-20 minutes," mom says. "Now sit back and enjoy the ride. Look out the window." The windows were rolled down—bringing in a rush of warm breeze.

"At what?" Tommy asks. "All I see out the window are cars, cars, and more cars. I've never seen this much traffic. Look, you can actually see steam rising from the pavement."

"Maybe they're all going to Riverview," Linda says. "Maybe it will be so crowded we'll never get on a ride."

"Maybe you're stupid! Do you know how big Riverview is? It could never get too crowded," Tommy says.

"Your sister is not stupid, Tommy. Don't talk to her like that."

"I didn't say she was stupid...I said **maybe** she was stupid."

Dad says, "And maybe I'll just turn this car around and we'll go home, since you kids aren't having any fun."

"Actually, dad, torturing Linda is fun. Anyway, she loves it. You love it, don't you Linda?"

Linda ignores him and asks, "What smells?"

Tommy has just removed a sock, and sticks his foot in Linda's face. "Maybe it's my foot."

"Mom, Tommy just put his crummy athletic foot on me. Yuck! No wonder you can't get in the pool half the time."

"It's not athletic foot. It's **athlete's** foot."

"I don't care what it's called. You've got a crummy fungus, is all I know."

"Kids, both of you, settle down right now. You're dad's trying to drive in all this traffic and he doesn't need you guys fighting."

Twenty minutes later. "How many more blocks to Belmont, dad?" Linda asks. "I'm boiling. I need something cold to drink or I'll die."

"We're at 1600 North," dad says. "Belmont Avenue is 3200

PROLOGUE

North. So you tell me, Linda, how many more blocks do we have to go? Tommy, don't tell the answer."

Linda starts to count, but then loses interest. She likes the name Belmont, and secretly wishes they lived on Belmont. It sounds much better than Hamlin. She didn't like the "ham" part of the word because it was a meat she didn't like. She likes the "lin" part of the word, though, because it was the first three letters of her name. How do streets get named? she wondered. Anyway, Belmont sounded cool, and if they lived on Belmont, they could go to Riverview any time they wanted. They could probably even walk to Riverview.

Tommy is thinking about his new pink shirt. He had been admiring it in the display window at Marks Toggery for weeks, and today he's wearing it for the first time. He loves this shirt. Next he wants to buy a pair of black pants that have a pink stripe down the length of each leg. In his mind he pictures himself walking through Riverview Park dressed in his new pink shirt and black pants with the pink stripes. People would pause to admire him, especially eighth grade girls. He then revises his daydream. He now pictures himself walking through Riverview in his new clothes, holding the hand of an eighth grade girl. He pictures a girl in his class named Barbara Rubins, but the name he gives her is Adele, and she is wearing a pink scarf around her neck, to match his shirt. Maybe they will go in the Tunnel of Love!

Linda's voice brings him back. "Twelve blocks to go, Tommy. We're at 2000 north. Just twelve more blocks. But where's the parachute ride?"

Riverview is the only amusement park to have a ride like the Pair-o-chutes. It's a tall structure, about 212 ft. high. As you sit two in a seat, strapped in with a lap belt that seems to offer little protection, an array of cables and pulleys propel you upward. As you reach the top, you pause in mid-air and then plunge downward, experiencing an 80 ft. free fall, before the chute fills with air slowing you down before you reach the bottom.

The previous year Tommy and Linda had gone to Riverview with mom and dad. They had said they wanted to go on the Pair-o-chutes, but Linda was having second thoughts as she stood watching the chutes go up and down, listening to all the screaming riders as they came down.

"It looks too scary to me," Linda said.

"Come on, Linda. It's not scary....it's thrilling. Please lets go on it. We'll be down before you know it."

After a little more coaxing, Linda reluctantly agreed. After a short wait in line, they got into the seat and once strapped in, they began the long ride upward, feet dangling, the seat swaying to and fro in the breeze. When nearing the top, Tommy turned around and said, "Hey, Linda, look behind you. You can see the Chicago River."

"Are you crazy?" she said, barely able to speak. "I'm not looking back."

"Linda, the reason this place is called Riverview is because

it's got this great view of the river. But you can only see the river from up here."

With that, he started rocking the chair back and forth until it seemed they would nearly tip over. Linda started screaming. Suddenly, as they were leaning way back, they hit the top and came plunging downward. It was a terrifying fall, and Linda could still recall the sickening feeling in her stomach. When they got off, Linda vowed she would never go on that ride with Tommy again. She never did see the Chicago River.

Just thinking about that experience last year, gets Linda angry all over again. "That was so mean of you," she says, reminding him just in case he didn't remember.

"That was a year ago. Get over it. You're such a chicken."

Dad, who had been fairly quiet, interjected. "No, she's not a chicken, Tommy. The pair-o-chute is a scary ride. Besides, she's almost two years younger than you. I don't know why you scare her like that."

Then dad says, "Hey, kids, look straight ahead." This is always the most thrilling moment in the long drive to Riverview—the sudden appearance of the slender steel structures jutting into the sky, with the six white chutes suspended from its arms. And the thought that people were actually up there, riding it at this very moment.

Arriving at the park, Tommy and Linda take each ride in order. They do the three coasters—the Blue Flash, the Silver Streak and the Greyhound in quick succession. They do the Silver

Streak twice. Standing in line at Shoot the Chutes—a hugely popular water ride—Tommy is eating a hot dog and Linda is holding a huge cone of pink cotton candy. Mom and dad are resting on a nearby bench, in the shade, sipping cold drinks. Loud speakers are blaring music. Brilliant colored lights flash and flicker on every ride and game booth. Everywhere you look there are hundreds of people yelling, laughing, running, hurrying to the next ride or game. The air smells of popcorn, peanuts, and motor oil. Screams are everywhere as coasters roar around the curves and hurdle down the dips...and then the ever-present click-click-click-click of the chains slowly pulling the coaster cars up the tracks...up up up...until the coaster comes to a momentary pause at the top...before plunging down a steep drop to the delighted shrieks of the riders.

"This is better than the St. Christopher carnival," Linda says.

"Yeah, just a little."

Standing in line, in the intense sun, Tommy and Linda, finally board Shoot the Chutes, from which they emerge, a few minutes later, thoroughly drenched, much cooler, and laughing. Then they scramble in line to ride again.

They play some of the booth games and some of the ball-throwing games. Tommy particularly likes Dunk the Drunk. In this game, a hobo or clown is seated on a wooden seat suspended above a tank of water. You are given three balls for a dime, and if you hit the bull's eye target, the seat drops from beneath the

PROLOGUE

clown and he disappears into the tank of water—emerging a few seconds later, soaked and scowling. But after nine balls, Tommy has yet to hit the target. The clown taunts him loudly, telling him he couldn't hit the broad side of a barn.

"Come on, Tommy," dad says. "You've spent enough money here."

"Just one more time, dad. Please."

Dad gives Tommy another dime. The first two balls miss. The clown continues his insults. Dad says, "Let me try the last ball, Tommy."

"Okay, dad, go ahead."

Dad winds up to the taunts of "Come on old man, I'll bet you can't even get the ball this far, you're too old and..." — in mid sentence, with mouth still flapping, the clown plunges into the tank. Tommy will never forget that sweet moment. But the next day he will tell friends that he was the one who dunked the drunk.

When they reached the Pair-o-chutes, Linda, true to her word, would not go on with Tommy. Dad had to do double duty, first going up with Tommy, then going back up with Linda. She actually enjoyed the ride that day with dad.

Tommy was eager to go on the Bobs, the fastest and highest roller coaster at Riverview, but since the Bobs were located at the rear of the park, it was one of the last rides they would go on. When they finally reached the Bobs, it was late in the day and the crowd had thinned.

Tommy hurriedly said, "Come on, Linda. Let's go. There's

no waiting."

"Not with you. If I go on it at all, I'm going with dad."

"Linda, I'm taking your mother on the Bobs. Go with Tommy. You'll be fine. Just hold on tight."

"No, I'm not going. It looks too scary."

"Come on, Linda. Last year you didn't go on them but said you would this year. You're such a baby. Wait until I tell everyone how you chickened out," Tommy cajoled.

That did it. Linda wasn't about to be called a baby. Against her better judgment, she muttered, "All right, let's go."

The Bobs, without a doubt, was the premier ride at Riverview, and the most feared, especially among first time riders. It was a classic wooden roller coaster comprised of 17 hills. The walk up the long steel ramp to the loading platform felt, to Linda, like the walk of death. With knees already wobbling, she and Tommy settled in their seat. Moments later the ride began. The climb upward to the top of the first hill seemed to take forever. Linda was terrified. She went flying half way out of her seat as they came thundering down the first steep drop. Hanging on for dear life, Linda kept repeating to herself, "It will be over soon, it will be over soon." All she wanted was to get off that ride. Tommy, meanwhile, with arms high in the air, was loving every minute of it. When the coaster finally pulled into the station, the attendant announced that anyone who wanted to stay on the ride, could do so for a dime. Linda, still recovering from the horror of the ride and trying to calm down, was totally

PROLOGUE

unaware when Tommy handed the attendant another 20 cents. Before she knew what was happening, the coaster, once again, had begun its slow ascent up that first treacherous hill.

"Let me off," she yells. But no one could hear her.

"Too late," Tommy said. "Here we go."

That day, Linda made a vow that she would never trust her brother at an amusement park again. Not ever!"

October 2002, I was sitting outside on the deck enjoying the last warmth of the fading sun. Two squirrels were scurrying around the yard, running up and down trees, one behind the other, as though they were playing follow the leader. The last of the leaves were falling steadily from the trees, and the late afternoon air was cool and damp. Indian summer was in its waning days, and another winter was just around the corner. As I sat there pondering whether I should go in and start dinner, I found myself with a growing restlessness. In just a few short weeks, I would turn 60. I can remember when my grandma turned 60, even when my mom turned 60, but *me* turning 60? I've never been one to let birthdays get me down. In fact, just the opposite. Every birthday I consider a blessing, but this one felt different, and lately I found myself more and more, as 60 neared, looking back on my life and remembering the childhood that I loved.

Later that night, still unable to shake this restless feeling, I started putting my thoughts on paper. The end result was a poem

I called "Turning 60." I always did like to recall moments from my youth and share them with my own kids when they were young, and now even more so with my grandkids, always wondering if they really understand the differences in the way my family lived compared to their life today.

What strikes me as the biggest difference between my generation and the generation of today's kids is that we played. We played for hours on end, using our imagination in everything we did. It took so little to make us happy. I can't ever remember saying the words "what's there to do?" or "I'm bored." In fairness to today's kids, maybe we, too, would have played less and used our imagination less if we had grown up with cable TV with its hundreds of channels, VCR's and DVD's, video games, computers, etc. We enjoyed the simple things, never needing fancy or expensive toys to amuse us. I'm not sure when this change started taking place, and while I try to keep an open mind so I don't become another *old* person who only dwells on the past, it's hard not to long for and remember a simpler time…

OUR TOWN

I was born in Chicago on October 31, 1942, (yes, Halloween), to Thomas and Elizabeth (Betty) Costello. They named me Linda May. I had one brother, Tommy, who was almost two years older than me, and I worshipped the ground he walked on. I was a very shy child, except at home. Then I was a non-stop chatterbox. I had an uncle who actually dubbed me "Chacharona," (talking machine). My memories of Chicago are dim. I know we had to flee one apartment because of cockroaches. We left another apartment because the landlord apparently did not like kids. At the age of three, we moved *far* away. At least that's what all of our relatives thought. The entire family, on both sides, lived on Chicago's North Side. For some reason, my dad bought an old home, a fixer-upper, about 25 miles south of Chicago, and probably about 50 miles from all the relatives. And because freeways and interstates had not been built yet, it was a very long drive. It is in that big house that the childhood I remember begins.

Hamlin Avenue

Markham, Illinois. It was a small country town, barely a dot on a map, if it was there at all. It wasn't a very pretty town, as towns go. Most roads were gravel, and that was the good roads. Many were just dirt roads, including the street I grew up on. Early on, homes were just built anywhere someone could get a piece of property. Most houses were of the Cape Cod style, not necessarily attractive, but most often very roomy. Later, several developments would be built. They did nothing to improve the town, other than give us new places to go trick-or-treating. The main street held the usual shops; Burrell's grocery store, with its big array of penny candy, a Rexall drug store with a soda fountain where we could get cherry cokes and green rivers, a gas station, and a few diners and bars. There were two schools: a grade school for first through fifth and a school for sixth through eighth, and the usual assortment of churches. I thought it was the greatest town in the world. Tommy and I grew up in this town. It was our town, and we loved it.

The neighborhood where we settled was very poor, although I don't think I realized it at the time. The surrounding homes were small and most of them were in poor condition. The families were uneducated, and few of the kids even went to high school. Nevertheless, most of them were nice neighbors and we got along well with them. There were lots of kids to play with, usually in our yard, because it was not only the nicest, but certainly the biggest.

The house we grew up in, on Hamlin Avenue, was a big old

house, sitting on an acre and a half of land, with lots of rooms. I had just turned three years old when we moved into this house and I would spend the next 16 years in that home. The house had three bedrooms upstairs, where Tommy and I slept, and a bedroom on the first floor for mom and dad. It had a big front porch with a swing, and a back porch that had mom's wringer washing machine on it. She didn't have a dryer and wouldn't get one for several years. In the summer, mom would hang the clothes out to dry; and in the winter she strung a clothesline in the hall upstairs to dry the clothes. Off the kitchen was an old stairway leading upstairs. It was dark and dingy, and all the boards creaked. Always in the back of my mind as I'd go running up the stairs was that one day they would all just come tumbling down, me included. Every Monday in the winter I would come home from school, go running upstairs to my room, only to get knocked in the face with a bunch of clothes. At night it was even worse. There was no lighting going up the stairway and none in the hallway either. It would literally be pitch black and every time I'd go up and down stairs, those darn clothes were there, smacking me around. I hated Mondays in the winter. The bedrooms did not have any doors on them and it never occurred to me to think they should (at least not until I was much older). There were lots of dark, spacious closets, actually, they were attics, that were quite scary, especially if someone would accidentally get locked in there! The one bathroom, on the main floor, didn't have a bathtub or hot water. Mom used to wash us in the kitchen in a huge metal tub, in full view of any aunt or uncle or neighbor who happened to be around. It was very hot and humid in the summer, and very cold in the winter. This was of course, before air conditioning, and for a while, even a furnace.

The house was heated with a coal stove that occupied a corner of the dining room. It adequately heated the downstairs, but in the winter, the upstairs would be cold. During those months, Tommy and I would have to sleep downstairs on the floor, in makeshift beds mom put together, near the coal stove to keep warm. Come springtime, we would once again be able to sleep upstairs in our rooms. And as cold as it would get up there in winter, it would get just as hot in the summer. On those exceptionally hot nights, Tommy and I would, once again, sleep downstairs. Instead of near the coal stove, though, we would lie on the floor in the sun parlor, off the living room, underneath the windows to keep cool. Despite its flaws, we loved this old house, and because it was bigger than most of our relatives' homes, it just seemed natural for most family gatherings to be at our house. And there were many.

Several years after we moved in, dad finally got a furnace installed. Out went the coal stove and the pile of coal in the garage. Now all the rooms would be warm, and Tommy and I could even sleep upstairs all winter. And with the newly installed furnace, we were able to put in a hot water tank. Mom wouldn't have to heat water in the big tubs on the stove for laundry and baths. She was so excited, as well she should be. We also got a bathtub, and I tell you, we never complained when she said "Time for baths, kids." One Saturday morning we woke up to find dad tearing down the back stairway. He said he was building us a new one. Instead of in the back of the house, off the kitchen, the new staircase was off the dining room, in the corner where the coal stove used to be, up to the second floor, in full view when you walked in the front door. It was a natural wood finish and it was newer than anything else in the house. We thought it was the most beautiful thing we ever laid eyes on. We used to play on those stairs as if it was a playground. I thought we were rich, what with all the new things in our house.

The yard was huge and there were two old barns in the back yard that had seen better days. The previous owners didn't use them for anything. They were empty, and they came with the house. When we moved in, the barns were filthy, full of cobwebs, spiders and all sorts of bugs, and the air had a dank, musty smell. I was scared to death to go in there. But after mom got through with them, they were clean as a whistle and became a great place to play. I would take my dolls out there and play house. On rainy days, Tommy and I would bring our toys out to the barn and play all day, or at least until the rain stopped. One night at supper, dad announced that he was going to raise chickens. While Tommy thought it sounded like fun, my first thought was "there goes my playhouse." But raise chickens we did! Dad purchased a dozen or so brooders and then a few hundred baby chicks, plus a couple of roosters. Mind you, dad was not a farmer, so a lot of this was hit and miss. But thankfully, for the chickens at least, it was mostly hit. I loved the baby chicks. They were soft and cuddly and had a wonderful smell to them. I would play with them and hold them, and sometimes I'd put some of them in my doll carriage and push them around. It did not take long, however, before these chicks grew up. Then they were no longer fun or cute…just work.

I still didn't mind them but I *hated* having to collect the eggs. It isn't as if it was my job exclusively to gather the eggs, but now and then, if mom was busy, she would have me do it. The eggs were always warm, and because they hadn't been washed off yet, there was usually some chicken poop on them, and half the time when I'd reach for an egg, a chicken would peck at my hand. That was on a good day. On a bad day, the roosters would chase me all over the pen and I wouldn't even be able to get to the eggs. One time I collected at least a dozen or more eggs. Knowing how pleased mom would be, I sauntered towards the gate, eager to show her the full basket. Just as I was almost out of the pen, a rooster came out of nowhere and started pecking at my leg ferociously. He chased me all around the pen, and the faster I ran, the faster he came at me and continued pecking. In a last ditch effort to get rid of him, I flung the basket of eggs at him, and while he dug his way out from under the basket and the broken eggs, I made my escape. Needless to say, I didn't please mom that day, and there were no eggs for breakfast in the morning.

As the chickens started laying more eggs than we could eat,

dad decided he would supplement the family income by selling them. After school and on Saturday mornings, when other kids were outside playing, Tommy and I were busy selling eggs. Mom and dad would load up our wagon with cartons of freshly gathered eggs and off we'd go selling them door to door. We had some steady customers who would always buy a dozen. Nothing like fresh eggs, straight from the hen, for a small price. And since that venture paid off so well, dad decided he would start selling the chickens. On Saturday mornings, dad would go out to the pen and pick out a dozen or so chickens. After killing them, he would bring them into the kitchen where mom would defeather, degut, and clean them, a very messy and smelly job. I tried to stay out of the kitchen on Saturday mornings. Once again, after the wagon was loaded, Tommy and I would go door to door peddling not only eggs, but chickens, as well. Unfortunately, people weren't quite as eager to buy chickens as they were eggs, especially from two young kids. After a few Saturday's of bringing back many unsold chickens, dad realized the chicken venture was not working out. Not only were we not making money, we were actually losing money because the unsold chickens had to be thrown out, all except for one which mom would fry up for supper on Sunday. We went back to just selling eggs.

Several years after the arrival of the first batch of chicks, we had a terrible flood in the area. All through the night, the heavy rains kept pounding away, and the next day, when it had finally stopped, dad waded in knee-deep water out to the barn, only to find that most of the chickens had drowned. We all felt terrible, not because we necessarily loved the chickens, but rather because of the awful way they died. Dad debated briefly whether to buy more chicks and start again, but in the end, I think he was as tired of them as Tommy and I were. He sold the brooders and other supplies and that was the end of our chicken business. Thank God! Once again, after mom got through scouring the barns, I had my playhouse back. And because I was older now, instead of playing with dolls, I would now use the playhouse to "pretend." Pretend I was a singer, or dancer, or actress. I was always sort of a ham and this was a great place for me to perform…where no one could see me. I'd sing for hours on end or act out scenes from a movie. Once in a while mom, or God forbid, a neighbor kid, would appear in the doorway while I was belting out a song. I'd feel so darn silly, but mostly embarrassed, that someone actually heard me singing.

OH, BROTHER

My brother Tommy was born on February 7, 1941 and named Thomas Leonard, after dad and Grandpa Molin, my mom's dad. As he got older, family and friends would start to call him Tom, but to me he is, and always will be, Tommy. From the day he was born, he was *everybody's* favorite. Grandma and Grandpa Molin had four daughters (Diane, Delores, Elizabeth and Inez), and while Grandpa wouldn't have traded one of them for all the tea in China, nevertheless, he longed for a son. When my dad told him the news about the baby being a boy, why you can just imagine his joy. He had a grandson. And when they gave him the middle name of Leonard, well, he was just bursting with pride. The story goes that he was so excited, the following day when he went to work he handed out cigars, not just to co-workers, but to any man he passed along the way to work, exclaiming loudly, "I have a son, I have a son!"

My aunts, mom's sisters, adored him, too. Having grown up in a house with all girls, Tommy was definitely special to all of them. And a beautiful baby he was. Mom said that everywhere she went, people would stop and fuss over him. I came along almost two years later, and I can safely assume that my arrival didn't herald the excitement of Tommy's arrival. My Aunt Dee (Delores) had a baby girl, Kerry, two months after I was born, and five years later my Aunt Di (Diane) had a baby girl, Janice. More girls! Tommy remained the only boy—the King. He would remain the only boy for almost 15 years till my Aunt Honey (Inez) had a son, George. And while everyone was thrilled to have another boy in the family, the fact is, by this time the novelty had worn off. He was just another baby we all loved. Tommy remained the King.

Tommy was also my mom's favorite. If he was dad's favorite, too, dad didn't show it. Now I know mom loved me, but there was absolutely no doubt in my mind, or anyone else's, that Tommy was special — her little boy. Oh, how she loved him. You may be thinking now that I would have been jealous and resented him, but the funny thing is, I didn't, for I, too, loved him. I looked up to him and thought I was the luckiest girl in the world to have him for a big brother. Like my dad, he had a delightful sense of humor. He had a way of saying things that if said by anyone else, probably wouldn't have been funny, but coming from him you just wanted to laugh. He could talk me into most anything because he just had this sweet, devilish way about him. Most of my young life was spent with him always playing tricks on me. And I think one could actually call some of them "cruel" tricks. At the moment these "cruel" tricks were occurring, I would be furious, but then he'd look at me and say, "Aw come on Linda, don't be mad. I didn't mean it. I'm sorry. I won't do it again." And silly me, I'd say, "Do you promise?" And with a twinkle in his eye, he'd say "Of course, I promise!" All would be forgiven until the next time.

There was never a dull moment with him around. Tommy was the most popular kid in the neighborhood, too, and when he started school, the same thing. All the girls thought he was so cute, and the boys just wanted to be one of his friends. Even the teachers were smitten with him. They were always telling mom what a great kid he was and how they loved having him in their class. Most of my girlfriends at one time or another had a crush on him. He was good looking, got good grades, was very outgoing, had excellent taste in clothes, and he even had a good voice (unlike mine). That was a big part of my childhood… living in Tommy's shadow. But I didn't mind. Over the years, when I'd repeat some of these stories, the obvious question was always why I would still think he's the greatest guy in the world. To this day, I probably can't answer that question to anyone's satisfaction, but to me it was very simple. He was my brother. I loved him, and I know he loved me. And for all the nasty things he would do, believe me, there were lots of nice things he did, too. The nicest thing is that he played with me. And played not just the "boy" things like cowboys and Indians, or baseball, but he played the things I liked, such as cut-out dolls and dressing up in mom's clothes. When there were no other kids around, we could play together all day.

The tent was a makeshift job, one of mom's large, discarded sheets, staked down by pieces of twig and secured at the top by a piece of rope tied to a large tree branch. In the dark, in the moonlight, an observer could have seen right through the thin material, could have seen Tommy and Linda sitting squat-legged on pillows in the tiny space, and crawling closer, could have heard their whispering and occasional laughter. The tent sat in the yard on the side of the house, just off the driveway. The kids had a flashlight, and inside the tent, Tommy and Linda could see nothing outside, nothing at all. And the only thing they could hear was the incessant sound of the crickets.

For weeks, since the start of summer vacation, Tommy and Linda had been pestering their mom to let them stay out all night in the tent, and for weeks she had refused. Her rule was 9:00. They *could stay out in the tent until 9:00 and then they had to come in the house. "But mom," they argued, "it barely just gets dark at 9:00. It's no fun until it gets real dark." "I don't care," mom countered. "I'm not going to lay awake all night long worrying about all the things that might happen to you kids in the middle of the night."*

Finally, though, they had worn her down, and today she said that if dad thought it was okay, she'd let them spend the whole night in the tent. The kids got so excited they could hardly wait — they even asked her if they could call him at work ("No!"), but they were so certain their dad would consent that they spent the remainder of the afternoon getting ready. They picked out games, books, snacks, drinks, and by the time dad's car was pulling in the driveway at 5:00, the tent was almost fully provisioned for the long, adventurous night ahead. Even before he could get into the house they had received his permission. "But if you kids get scared in the middle of the night," mom said, "don't come running in the house screaming. Your dad has to get up for work in the morning."

Now it was a little after 11:00. In the darkness, Tommy and Linda saw the lights in the house go out, meaning that mom and dad had gone to bed. For the past two hours they had been having fun just soaking up the newness of it all. The very idea that they would be out here, in the dark, throughout the night — that inside the house their beds would remain empty — it all seemed kind of dreamlike. Several times they had left the tent and sneaked through the grass to the Brandy yard next door, and had peaked in their windows, finding nothing exciting to look at — but just the act of looking was exciting.

Back in the tent the kids had eaten their snacks and then Tommy had started telling scary stories. They had agreed to keep the flashlight turned off. His plan had been to get his sister so terrified that she'd throw in the towel and retreat to her bedroom, but so far she was holding her own and even seemed to be enjoying the sense of fear and danger lurking out in the darkness. For his part, Tommy was already tired of the tent and longed for the comfort of his own bed, but he could never admit this to Linda. Also, his own nerves were getting a little shaky. A moment ago he would have sworn he heard a rustling just outside the tent—he even looked up at Linda to see if there was any sign of heightened alertness on her face. But she seemed absorbed in his story about a boy who suffered curious side effects from staring too long at the moon. Staring at the moon had caused one side of his face to cave in, just like Iggy Wotasik. Staring at the moon made the boy sing "I Never Knew the Gun was Loaded" hundreds of times a day. Finally when the boy grew up he shot and killed the woman who wrote that song. But that didn't end it. Sentenced to 60 years in prison, he continued to sing "I Never Knew the Gun was Loaded" until one day a fellow inmate could stand it no longer and put a very loaded gun to his head and finally silenced him forever.

"I don't really believe this story," Linda said. "You're just making it up and anyway it's not very scary."

"Prove to me that you don't believe it," Tommy told her.

"How do I prove it?" she asked.

"Go outside the tent and stand in the yard and stare at the moon for 10 minutes."

"I'm not going out there in the dark, by myself. For 10 minutes. Do you think I'm crazy?"

"What I think is that you're afraid your face will cave in like

Iggy Wotasik's and that you'll sing "I Never Knew the Gun—"

Linda interrupted: "Why don't YOU go outside and stare at the moon for 10 minutes, if you're so brave."

"Because I believe the story," Tommy said. "You're the one who says she doesn't believe it."

Linda plopped down on her back. "I'm getting tired," she said. "Let's go to sleep."

Tommy lay down on the pillow and stretched out. They lay there for a few minutes in silence.

"Isn't this fun?" Linda asked.

"The most fun I've ever had in my life," Tommy said.

"Are you a little scared?" she asked.

"Oh yeah, just terrified," he said, sarcastically.

Then, they both heard it and they sat upright and stared at each other.

"What was that?" Linda said. "Tommy, did you hear that?"

"Yes. It sounded like knuckles cracking."

"Or twigs snapping," she said. "Tommy, go out there and look around."

"It was probably just some bum who escaped from the Manteno nut house" he said. "If you're scared, maybe you should go in the house."

"I'm not going in the house unless you do," she said.

"I'm not going in, this is too much fun," Tommy said.

"Please go out there and look around," she asked.

"I'm too tired," Tommy pleaded. "I'm going to sleep."

They lay down again in silence. After a few minutes, Linda said: "I just know someone is out there, I just know it."

"Maybe it's Russell Yonda," Tommy said.

Earlier, after supper, while Tommy and Linda were getting the tent ready for their adventure, Tommy's friend Russell Yonda had come by on his bike to see if Tommy wanted to do something. When they told him of their plans to stay out in the tent all night long, he had expressed great interest, and Linda later said she thought Russell was hoping they would invite him to join them. But when, after about a half hour, while Tommy and Linda kept making trips back and forth from tent to house and back, Russell finally got on his bike and went home.

Tommy yelled out into the darkness: "Are you out there, Russell Yonda?" Linda tried to pull a pillow over his face. "Shhhhh," she said.

They listened in silence for a few moments, then lay down again. "I've never really liked Russell Yonda very much if you want to know the truth," Linda said. "He's the weirdest of all your friends."

"You're still mad at him because of the ice cream cone," Tommy said. A few weeks ago, Linda had been walking home from the drug store in Markham that had a great soda fountain. She had an ice cream cone in her hand and was walking alone down the street, when Tommy and Russell Yonda approached from behind, on their bikes. Linda had no idea they were coming up from behind. She was just walking along down the shady

street, all by herself, enjoying the beautiful weather and her ice cream cone, when Russell sped by on his bike and reached out and slapped the cone right out of Linda's hand. The cone fell on the hot black asphalt and the pink ball of ice cream melted in minutes. Linda had stopped, startled, and glared at the boys as they raced down the road and disappeared around the corner. Tommy had glanced back once and when he saw his sister standing there in the street, staring down at the fallen cone, he felt a sudden anger at Russell, and felt sorry for his sister. Later, he wished he had turned around and gone back and offered to ride back to the drug store and buy her another cone. Thinking about it now, he wondered again why he had not acted on that impulse. It had been very mean of Russell Yonda.

"Of all my friends, he's the one I like least," Tommy said. "Sometimes he can be okay, but he really bugs me a lot. None of my other friends can figure out why I hang around with him."

Outside the tent, a solitary figure lay crouched in the dark, listening, breathing, occasionally cracking knuckles. He waited patiently. He heard Tommy tell Linda he was going to run in the house to go to the bathroom. He waited, listening to Linda talk to herself as the minutes went by: "What could he be doing in there?" "How could it take this long to pee?" And then he started breathing, deep sighs of breath, and he cracked a knuckle. And he watched Linda bolt from the tent, run up the front porch steps and into the house.

Inside, Linda found her mom in the kitchen. "Had enough?"

her mom asked.

"Where's Tommy?"

"He went to bed. He said you wanted to sleep outside all night by yourself."

"Mom! He told me he had to go to the bathroom and he'd be right back. I've been waiting for half an hour! I've been sitting out there alone in that tent, in the dark, and I keep hearing strange breathing and the sound of cracking bones or twigs."

"That brother of yours," mom laughed.

"That brother of mine?" Linda nearly screams. "Is that all you can say? He left me alone outside, and all you do is laugh about it? You ought to go upstairs and smack him silly!"

"Come on, Linda, settle down. I wouldn't have let you stay out there all night by yourself. Now go on up to bed."

The next day, Tommy and Linda were out in the yard cleaning the tent of the debris from the night before. Linda was still mad. Tommy kept apologizing, saying he was sorry and that he'd never do that again. He wanted to play cutouts and then get on the boxing gloves as soon as the tent was clean. It wouldn't be fun if Linda was in a bad mood. Then he looked up and saw Russell Yonda coming around the corner on his bike at a pretty good clip. Tommy stood up and started to wave at him, but Russell Yonda never slowed down and never even looked in his direction. Tommy and Linda looked at each other, and then watched Russell Yonda recede in the distance.

Behind our house were miles of open field. One day a tractor came and carved out a long ditch a block behind our house. We never did find out why it was dug out like it was, or who dug it, but that ditch, which consisted of a wonderful moist, sandy soil, became our summer playground for years. We brought our shovels and little toy cars and we carved out elaborate streets and constructed houses and made little rivers and lakes. Some days we would get to the ditch first thing in the morning and stay all day until mom called us home for supper. Now and then during the day, I'd leave to run back to the house for a few minutes to go to the bathroom (Tommy just used the field) or to bring us back something to eat and drink. This one particular day, I had really been working hard building the most elaborate roadway and houses. It looked like a small village. After proudly looking at my handy work, I told Tommy I'd be right back. I was gone about 10 minutes. When I returned with snacks, my entire little village was raked perfectly flat. I couldn't believe it. I stood there frozen, unable to move or speak. When I finally recovered from the shock, I went racing back to the house crying. Mom came out and asked what was wrong. "Tommy ruined the entire village I just built, just to be mean," I said. "Oh, I can't believe he'd do a thing like that. You must be mistaken. Come on," she said, "let's go." We walked back to the ditch, and when she saw the flattened area, down from where his beautiful village remained, she got very upset, too. "Tommy, did you ruin Linda's village?" "Honestly, mom, I swear I had nothing to do with it. I left the ditch just for a few minutes to go into the field and go to the bathroom, and when I came back, there it was...wrecked by some unknown meanie. I feel just terrible. All her hard work for nothing."

"See Linda, I knew there had to be a simple explanation. Tommy would never be that mean," she said. Mom actually *believed* him. But I didn't. I knew the truth.

One of my fondest childhood memories is the good times I had with my cousin, Kerry. We had lots of cousins on both sides of the family, but Kerry was my favorite. In addition to seeing her several times throughout the year, for a number of summers, Kerry would come out and spend a month or two at our house. Those were the best summers for me. As much as I loved my brother, having Kerry to play with every day was great. She was only two months younger than me and it was like having a sister. She was an only child so she also enjoyed spending summers with us. Tommy loved it, too. If playing tricks on one girl was fun, imagine having two girls around to tease. Not only did Kerry and I get along great, but she was crazy about Tommy, too. In fact, many years later, she told me that when she was a young girl, she used to think that when they grew up, she would marry Tommy.

One Easter Sunday, Kerry came out with her parents. She brought with her a baby chick someone had given her. She named her Chirpy. She didn't know what to do with this baby chick, and since we were raising chickens at that time anyway, she asked if she could leave Chirpy with us, and asked me to take care of her. I was thrilled. We put Chirpy in the pen with the rest of the chicks. She sort of blended in but I knew which one she was. For the next month or so I took good care of Chirpy. Tommy would tease me for having a chicken for a pet. I told him he was just jealous that Kerry gave Chirpy to me and not to him. Now I know this sounds silly, but I swear Chirpy knew who I was. Every time I'd go in the pen, most of the chickens would scurry away, the roosters would just try to peck at me, but Chirpy would just sort of saunter around, and she'd even let me pick her up. Now and then I'd put her in our wagon and pull her around. She didn't even seem to mind that, although after a few minutes she would jump out. At least once a week, Kerry would call and ask how Chirpy was doing. I would, of course, tell her Chirpy was doing just fine, getting big and plump. She couldn't wait for school to get out so she could come out and spend the summer with me… and Chirpy.

One Sunday morning, dad went out to the pen to get us a nice chicken for supper. Tommy went with him and together they looked around for a nice big one. As a big plump one came scampering by, dad said, "Hey, this looks like a good one." With a mischievous look in his eye, Tommy quickly agreed. "Yeah, dad, she's perfect. I'll get her for you." And off he went, chasing the chicken all over the pen. The more he chased it, the faster the chicken ran. "Hey Tommy," dad said, "there are plenty of other plump chickens. Forget that one and grab any one of them."

"No, this one really looks good," he insisted. After a few more attempts, he finally caught her. With chicken in tow, they left the pen where dad promptly got his axe and chopped off its head. (I know that sounds awful but that's how it was done.) He brought the chicken in to mom for cleaning and cooking. Later that day, mom called us in for supper. We're at the table eating and talking. Just as I picked up the drumstick and started to take a bite, I suddenly heard Tommy very faintly start chanting "Chirp, Chirp, Chirp." And in that instant, I knew….it was Chirpy, all fried up and ready to eat. I threw the drumstick down and started crying. Mom asked what was wrong and I told her. Boy, were they mad at Tommy. Dad said he had no idea that the chicken Tommy handed him was Chirpy. When Tommy realized just how upset I was, he apologized — over and over. "Honest, Linda, I really didn't know you'd be this mad. I wouldn't have done it, I swear." He went on to say that he just didn't think of a chicken as a pet and thought it was just a funny thing to do. Still crying, I said, "Well, I wonder if you'll still think it's funny when I tell Kerry what you did!" I really do think he felt bad and was sorry, but I was still too mad to forgive him, at least not immediately. I didn't talk to him the rest of the day…I didn't eat chicken for months.

Tommy and Linda are sitting in the bus stop at 159th Street and Brennan Highway. It's about 100 degrees in the shade. The bus stop has a roof and is open in the front. There is no floor.

Tommy and Linda have walked the six blocks from their house, following a path diagonally through the field. Their destination is the Harvey swimming pool.

They are sitting side by side with their backs against the wall of the bus stop and their legs straight out in front of them. They are wearing shorts. Tommy has taken off his T shirt and is using it as a fan.

"How long until the bus?" Linda asks. Tommy looks at his watch. "It's ten-to-two," he says. "Ten more minutes."

"What if it's late?" Linda asks.

"Whaddaya mean what if it's late? If it's late, it's late. We have to wait, that's all."

"What if it was early and we missed it?" she asks.

"It's never early."

"No, Doris Willmer said she got to the bus stop right on time once and saw the bus pulling away."

"That's not early, that's right on time."

"I just want to get in the water. This heat is awful. I feel like I'm on fire."

The bus stop sits back from the highway about two car lengths. Tommy and Linda sit on the ground and watch the heat rise up from the pavement. There isn't even a hint of a breeze. Every few minutes a car zooms by stirring up dust. This intersection of 159th and Brennan has no stop sign, and there is nothing else in sight but flat, empty fields. The nearest shopping district in Markham is a mile down the road, and the larger town of Harvey is another four miles beyond Markham. Tommy and Linda have made this trip a hundred times, but never on a day as hot as this one.

Linda sits on the ground and pictures her mother in the back yard hanging clothes on the line. The heat will not deter her mom. Nothing gets in the way of her housework.

"Tommy, get up and check to see if the bus is coming."

"We'll hear it coming, I'm not moving until it gets here."

"But you could at least check to see if it's anywhere in sight yet."

"If you want to know so bad then you get up and check. I'm not budging. It's too hot out there in the sun."

"Yeah, well it's not exactly a cooler in here either. I feel like we're sitting in an oven." She pictures their kitchen oven and wonders what it would feel like to be a loaf of bread.

"I wish I had a popsicle," she says.

"I wish you had a cup of hot chocolate," Tommy tells her.

"Now that's mean. I'm going to tell ma."

"Yeah, and I'm going to tell her you didn't wear your glasses in school for months."

"Yeah, and I'm going to tell her you tried to give me your athlete's foot disease."

"It's not a disease!"

"Yeah, well they might not even let you in the pool," Linda taunts. On two or three occasions over the past few summers, Tommy was told by the pool attendant he couldn't enter the water because of his athlete's foot rash. At that time, every kid had to

step into a square basin of water that contained some kind of disinfectant, and then the attendant checked everyone's feet. Tommy hated this moment. If he had to sit on the pool deck on a day like this one, he'd fry.

"What time is it?" Linda asks again.

Without answering, Tommy stands up and walks out to the highway and stands by the sign that says: BUS STOP. He peers down the road. Nothing in sight. "God is it hot out here," he says. "If I don't get in that pool pretty soon I'm going to fry. I'll bet it's going to be packed." He walks back and plunks down on the ground next to his sister.

Linda grabs his wrist and studies his watch. "It's five minutes to two," she says. "That's if your watch is right."

"It's right all right."

"It's going to be late," Linda says. She remembers that Uncle George always told them: "A good bus driver always gets there on time." Uncle George had been driving a bus in Chicago for 30 years. He had the exact same route his entire life: the Fullerton to Pulaski to Belmont line. Once Tommy had asked him if he didn't get bored driving the same streets over and over. "Not for a minute," George told him. "I love that route. I like seeing the same people — some of them have been riding my bus for 20 years. I know about their families. They send me a Christmas card. That's because I talk to them — and I always try to be on time."

Linda says, "Wouldn't it be neat if Uncle George had this

route?"

"Yeah," Tommy says. "I bet he'd let us ride for free." Tommy and Linda liked Uncle George a lot. He was fun and he always told them stories, usually bus stories. They almost never saw him when he wasn't wearing his uniform. When he was a young man, he was in the Navy, and there are pictures of him wearing his Navy whites and a big grin.

Linda pictured the Harvey pool. She could see in her mind exactly how it would look when they got there. That first wonderful sight of the beautiful blue water. Hundreds of kids laughing, squealing, and splashing. The pungent smell of the chlorine. The way the water felt when you first jumped in—a slight shock to the system that always made you yelp with delight. Mom said they had to be home no later than 5:00, when dad would be pulling in the driveway and supper would be on the table. That would give them more than two hours to swim.

"That water is going to feel soooo good," Linda says.

"I hope Donna Walker isn't there," Tommy says. "The pool is always too crowded when she's there." Donna Walker was a neighbor, a few years older, and the fattest girl in school.

"That's not nice, and I'm telling mom you said that."

A truck roars by stirring up a lot of dust, and then a dog appears on the other side of the highway. It seems to look both ways, then slowly limps across the pavement and stops right under the bus stop sign. This dog has seen better days. It regards Tommy and Linda sitting in the bus stop, then it starts down the highway.

"He looks hungry and thirsty," Linda says. "I wish we had something to give him."

"I'm hungry and thirsty," Tommy says. "I wish we had something to give US."

"He looks sad and lost," Linda says.

"He actually looks like he's waiting for the bus," Tommy says. "Well, he'll have to sit in the back of the bus."

Now in the distance they could hear the sound of a motor.

"That sounds like a bus motor, Tommy. Go see if that's the bus coming."

"I'm not budging until I see that bus parked right here. Hey, dog, is that the bus coming?"

The dog clearly saw the bus coming. They watch it limp backward, several steps away from the highway, they hear the roar of the motor, they feel vibration in the ground and in the air around them, and then they see the big red and white bus fly by in a cloud of dust. Tommy and Linda both jump up and race out to the highway. Tommy runs into the middle of the highway and starts jumping up and down and waving his arms. "What the hell... STOP, you idiot. STOP!" But by this time the bus is a football field away.

Tommy and Linda stare at one another in disbelief. "He didn't even slow down," Tommy says.

"That's because he didn't see us," Linda says. "He didn't see us because we were sitting way at the back of the bus stop. I told *you to go see if that was the bus."*

Tommy says: "Why is it called a bus stop? Do you know why it's called a bus stop. Because it's a place where the damn bus is supposed to stop."

"I'm telling mom you swore," Linda says. "Twice."

"Damn damn damn damn damn damn..." Tommy says. "How many times is that?"

Tommy and Linda stare down the road at the disappearing bus, then they cross the pavement and head to the path toward home in the sweltering heat. They don't say much. They are hot and thirsty, and the thought that there would be no Harvey pool for them today is almost too much to bear. As they walk, they both keep thinking about the unfairness of it all. They had done nothing wrong. They were just two kids waiting for the bus, and for no reason at all this bus driver decided not to stop at the bus STOP. If they had been told by some adult, some time in the past, that you cannot trust bus drivers to always stop at a bus stop, then it might be partly their fault for not listening to this cautionary statement. But no adult had ever told them any such thing, not even Uncle George. So, Tommy and Linda learned something important that day. Adults can't always prepare them for all of the things that will happen in life. There are some things that happen in life they will have to find out for themselves.

Behind them, the dog limped along the path and followed them all the way home. Where they were all treated to water, food, and sympathy.

One Sunday morning mom and dad were busily preparing for our annual picnic. They called it Coselinski Day. Since we were Italian, I had no idea how or why the name Coselinski came to be. Sometimes as a child, you simply accept things as they are. In later years I learned that because dad had told some of the guys he worked with that Costello wasn't really his last name, one of the guys said, "Hey, maybe you're not really Italian either." Another piped up with, "Yeah, maybe you're Polish—maybe you're really Coselinski."

Somehow, a few weeks later when dad told everyone at work that he was going to have a big picnic at his house, someone quickly interjected, "You mean Coselinski Day?" and from then on, because dad had a great sense of humor, and because we didn't live in an era of political correctness, the name lived on for as long as he had the yearly event. Anyway, once a year dad would invite all the people he worked with to our house to spend a day in the country. Most of them were city folk living in apartments and they loved coming out to our place. In addition to tons of food mom would prepare, there was lots to do. We owned the vacant lot next to us and everyone would join in to play baseball, have races, hit golf balls, play badminton, or anything else that came to mind. The guys would sit around late in the day, drink beer, smoke cigars, while the ladies would help mom clean up some of the mess. It was a day we always looked forward to every year.

On the day of the picnic, mom, after giving both Kerry and me a bath in the big old metal wash tub, dressed us in new sun dresses she had made, fixed our hair, put on freshly polished shoes, and then told us to go outside and wait for company to arrive. As we ran outside she hollered, "And whatever you do, don't you dare get dirty." We promised we wouldn't. "I know you girls, you always manage to, so I'm warning you, if you get your clothes dirty, I'll send both of you upstairs and you will not come down until everyone leaves. Not even to eat. And I mean it. Now tell Tommy to come in for his bath, right now!" Outside we found him in the garage playing in the coal pile (we hadn't gotten the new furnace yet). He asked if we wanted to join him and of course, we said no. "We can't, not today. We just got all cleaned up. Mom said we'll have to spend the entire day in our room if we get dirty." "Yeah," Kerry chimed in. "I think Aunt Betty really means it." So he started talking about how much fun he is having rolling in all the coal, and it really did look like fun. We didn't want to get too close to the coal pile, but he kept talking to us. When we'd answer him, he'd say he couldn't hear us and could we move in a little closer. The more he talked, the closer we started moving toward him. When we got next to him, he said "Here catch," and before we knew what happened, he tossed a piece of coal to each of us. We caught it and threw it back. Once again he threw the coal back to us and before we knew it, we were in the midst of a coal fight.

Inside the house, mom was waiting for Tommy to come inside for his bath. Through the open window in the kitchen, she could hear the three of us laughing and figured she better go outside and get Tommy herself. By the time she came into the garage, Kerry and I were buried in coal from head to toe. I don't know if I can adequately describe my mom's anger at that point. All I know for sure is that she pulled Kerry and me out of the coal, gave us both a smack on our behinds and dragged us into the house. After heating more water on the stove, she gave us another bath and sent us up to our room. True to her word, she would not let us come downstairs the entire day no matter how much we begged, cried, and said we were sorry. Late in the day she did come upstairs and bring Kerry and me each a small plate of food, with no dessert. As for Tommy, well, he told mom he had no idea why we would play with coal after being all cleaned up. And of course, after his bath, he got to go to the picnic. We'd look out the bedroom window from time to time and see him running and playing with the other kids, eating everything in sight, and having a great time. Occasionally, he'd see us peering out the window and he'd smile and wave to us. Now and then he would come upstairs to tell us what fun we were missing, and how stuffed he was from eating all that delicious food.

Father Knows Best

Dad's parents were born and raised in Guardia Lombardi, Italy in the Province of Avellino. He was one of eight children born to Gaetano (Guy) and Carmella Castellano. While still in Italy, their daughter Donna was born. When Donna was about two years old, they had another daughter named Isabella. Shortly after Isabella's birth, they had an opportunity to come to America. Because it would be such a long and arduous voyage crossing the Atlantic, and because grandma wasn't feeling well and unable to nurse Isabella, it was decided that Isabella would stay in Italy with my grandfather's sister, Concetta, who was able to nurse her. After grandma and grandpa were settled in America, and when they saved some money, they would send for Isabella. They settled in Pennsylvania in a small mining town called Tower Hill. There my grandfather worked as a coal miner. The work was long and hard, and money was scarce. They were in this country about two years when they were finally able to contact the relatives in Italy and said they were ready to bring

Isabella to her new home. They already had two more babies by then, Mary and George, but grandfather had somehow managed to save a little money and said he would send them the money if one of them would bring Isabella safely to America. The return letter was startling, to say the least. After caring for Isabella for two years, Concetta loved the little girl and had become very attached to her. She would not send her to America! The news was devastating and, unfortunately, Grandfather could not afford to go over there himself and get her. He needed to stay here and work. There were already many mouths to feed and clothe. He always vowed that someday he would go back and bring her home with him. However, it wasn't meant to be. Times were getting rougher, and still more babies came along: Frank, Bill, Thomas (dad), Charles and Ada. When my dad was five years old, and just 19 days after his youngest sister, Ada, was born, his dad died of black lung disease. Now raising all these children was left solely up to their mother. There was no way Isabella would ever get to join her family. She would spend her entire life in Italy. When she was much older, she was told of her family in America, and though none of our family ever got to meet her, several family members who could read and write Italian, did correspond with her.

After my grandfather's death, George, the oldest son, went to work in the coal mines. He was the sole source of income for the family. There also seemed to be quite a bit of confusion concerning their last name, Castellano. In school, the teachers all seemed to spell their name differently, and pronounce it differently. One of the boys was listed as Costello. The older family members decided they would change the name legally from Castellano to Costello to avoid further confusion. I'm still not quite sure why they did that, but frankly, I wish they hadn't. I would love to have been a Castellano. Sounds more Italian. After working in the mines for a number of years, George realized if they stayed in Tower Hill, his four younger brothers would eventually end up working in the mines, too. He wanted a better life for them, so he convinced his mom they had to move. They packed up the family and moved to Chicago to be near her sister. Dad's family became friends with a family called the Molin's, and on one visit when dad went along, he met one of the daughter's, Diane. He went out with her a few times, but Diane was also seeing a guy by the name of George Morsi. After a short time, she started seeing George exclusively, and would end up marrying him. Dad continued to visit the Molins and eventually he and mom started dating. After high school graduation, dad wanted very much to go to college, but he needed to work. Three of his brothers were already in the armed forces serving in World War II, and it was up to dad to help provide for his mom and youngest sister who was still living at home. He got a job as a time study clerk at Automatic Transportation (which later would become Eaton, Yale and Towne Corp.) and he would remain with them his entire life, working his way up to Industrial Engineer.

After a brief courtship, mom and dad married. A year later,

Tommy was born, and 20 months later I arrived. After moving into the Markham house, dad and mom settled into a very routine way of life. In fact, everything about dad was routine. He was definitely a creature of habit. You could almost plan an entire calendar year on what he would do. He *never* missed work. Every day he'd leave the house at precisely the same time, and would arrive home at the same time, give or take a few minutes. Some nights Tommy and I would go upstairs and look out the window in the hall. We could see all the way to Brennan Highway, which was probably about six blocks from our street. That's the road dad would be coming home on. Every time a car would come into view, we'd get excited and think maybe it was him, and eventually it would be dad. In the summer time, now and then, we would walk up to Brennan Highway to wait for dad. When he saw us he'd stop the car and let us get in, and continue the drive home. About a block before our house, dad would stop the car and let us out. We'd hop on the running board of the car and he'd drive the rest of the way home like that. We loved to do that, even more so if neighborhood kids were outside and saw us. Then we'd run as fast as we could into the house to tell mom that dad was home. Every night when he got in the house, he would hand Tommy and me each a half stick of Wrigley Spearmint gum — never once a whole stick, and never once Doublemint or Juicy Fruit or any other kind. And then he would always say, in case we didn't remember, "Save the gum for after supper." We were thrilled to get the gum, just as much as the previous night.

Off our kitchen was a breakfast nook, a very cozy room, painted a bright cheerful yellow, and we had all our meals in there, unless, of course, we had company. Then we ate in the dining room. Dad sat at the same spot every night at the table and every night he had some Gonnella Italian bread with his supper. "There is no meal if there is no bread," he often said. And along with the bread was a glass of red wine, usually a wine he had made. Conversation was a big part of our evening meal, every one going on about their day. It was something we all enjoyed. After supper he would go to the sun parlor where we had a piano, and there for a half hour, no more, no less, he would play his heart out. He *loved* the piano. I remember so many nights when I would sit along side him on the piano bench, he would play and I would sing. What great fun it was. Tommy and I both thought he was the greatest piano player in the world, but in reality, he was probably just fair—but it didn't matter, he loved playing the piano and we loved listening to him play. There was a song back then called "Linda" and dad would play the piano and sing that song to me. He also taught both of us to play the piano and read music. When the half hour was up, he would then go into the living room, or the front room as we called it, to watch television. At 10 p.m. he would watch the local newscast, and then go to bed, only to get up the next day and start all over again. And I would look forward to the following night when, once again, we would get to hear him play the piano.

On Friday nights, our neighbor, George Walker, would come

by driving his old red pickup truck. He would pick dad up and together they would go to the local liquor store and buy a pint of Early Times and a six pack of beer. Once in a while, on a warm summer night, dad would let Tommy and me go with them. Mr. Walker would let us sit in the back of the pickup which was always fun to do. After making their purchases, dad would buy a quart of Canfield's orange soda for Tommy and me (whether we went along for the ride or not) — never strawberry or root beer, or Coke or Pepsi — just orange. We were thrilled to get the soda. After returning to our house, dad and Mr. Walker would sit at the table in the breakfast nook and drink three cans of beer each, have a few shots of the whiskey, and talk while they discussed politics, their jobs, and the world in general. Mom would make popcorn for Tommy and me, to go along with the orange soda. Dad loved to philosophize, and they'd talk for several hours until dad fell asleep at the table. Mr. Walker would finish his beer, then get up, get in his pickup and drive the hundred yards to his home. Mom would wake dad up and tell him to go to bed. He would, and so began another weekend. On Fridays when Mr. Walker didn't stop by, dad would watch the Friday night fights on television and we would get to stay up and watch it with him. Mom would still make us popcorn, but we didn't have the orange soda. We got Kool-Ade instead. We loved it best when Mr. Walker came by.

Saturday mornings dad would go into the neighboring town of Blue Island to do our weekly banking. At the time, Markham did not have its own bank. He would drive to Blue Island, do the banking, then stop at the Long Bar to have a beer and place a bet on a horse. He loved horse racing. Once in a while he would let Tommy and me go with him to Blue Island. He'd usually give us a little money, maybe 50 cents each, and while he did the banking and went to place his bet, we'd look around. For a while, my Aunt Honey worked behind the soda fountain at the Woolworth's, and on those Saturdays when we'd go with dad, we couldn't wait to go in there. We'd sit at the counter and have her wait on us. And if she was working, we wouldn't have to spend our own money because she wouldn't charge us. After eating, we'd still have our 50 cents to spend.

When I was very young dad drove an old Dodge, but in 1949 he bought a brand new Nash. It was black and the ugliest car I had ever seen. We used to call it the "bathtub" or "tub" for short. He *loved* it. He talked about that car constantly, always saying what a fine sturdy car it was. I frankly was embarrassed even to be seen in it. I remember my friends' dads having really cool cars. There I was, being driven around in the "tub." One winter evening we were going to my Aunt Dee's house. My Aunt Honey, Uncle George, and year old Georgie came with us, too. It was a fairly mild January afternoon when we left home. Along the way it started to rain, and by the time we left Aunt Dee's for the long drive home, the temperature had dropped considerably and the roads had become a sheet of ice. We were at a stoplight when the car behind plowed into us. We were very fortunate none of us were hurt. But the Nash, for all its sturdiness, didn't fare so well. Luckily, we were able to drive it the rest of the way home, but the damage looked pretty extensive. The next day, after taking the car to Lee, his favorite mechanic, for an assessment of the damages, dad said the car was beyond repair and that he'd have to buy another car. Tommy and I were ecstatic!! The tub was gone. For the next few days after work, he went from car lot to car lot trying to find a good deal on another car. Tommy and I, of course, offered our opinions on the type of car he should get. After the "tub," we wanted something really cool. Finally, about a week after the accident, he said he had found one he liked. When he left to pick it up, we were all excited. "I hope it's a souped-up Chevy," Tommy said. "What kind do you hope it is?" he asked. "As long as it's not black, or a Nash, I don't care," I said. Finally, the moment we had been waiting for arrived. Dad pulled into the driveway honking the horn. We came out of the house running, even mom, all excited to see it. And there it was — another Nash. A 1954 black Nash with a little red thrown in (like that would make it better). It was just about as ugly as the "tub." "It's a fine car," dad said beaming. "Just as good, if not better, than the old '49." I wanted to cry. Tommy and I turned and headed back for the house. "Hey, kids, don't you want to check out the new car, maybe go for a ride?" dad asked. We didn't.

It is a little after 5 pm on a warm spring evening. Dad has just come home from work and now we're all at our places at the supper table. In our house, we never called supper "dinner," as so many people do today. One of the most popular radio shows of that era was not called "dinnertime frolic" — it was suppertime frolic — which mom listened to religiously every evening while preparing supper. On this night she made a meat loaf with mashed potatoes and gravy. Suddenly, there's someone at the front door, yelling "Mr. Costello! Mr. Costello! Come quick." It's Dennis Brandy, the neighbor boy. We all get up from the table and rush into the living room.

"What is it, Dennis?" mom asks.

"I think you should know that there's a lot of smoke coming out the window of Mr. Costello's car," Dennis says. He backs up so that we can open the screen door and come outside. Sure enough, there in the driveway is dad's beloved 1954 black and red Nash Ambassador with a blue smoke puffing out the back seat window.

Dad says, "How the hell! I just pulled in the driveway 15 minutes ago and my car wasn't on fire. What did you do, Dennis?" Dad runs outside and flings open the rear door. The fire seems to be located in the back seat, though you can't really see fire. The seat is just smoldering.

"I didn't do any thing," Dennis says, "except come over when I noticed the smoke."

Mom scolds dad. "Tom, how can you think Dennis would

start a fire in your car? That's not very nice."

"Personally, I think Dennis did it," Tommy says. "I always said he'd be an arsonist some day." Dennis sticks out his tongue at Tommy. Linda wants to know what an arsonist is.

Dad says, "Well, somebody must have started it, and Dennis is the only human being I see." He rushes into the garage, grabs a bucket, fills it with water, returns to the car and dumps the whole thing into the back seat. Within minutes, the smoke is gone, replaced by an unpleasant smell. Mom comes over and puts her head into the back seat. She reaches in and picks up a clump of wet pipe ash.

"Tom, you were smoking your pipe on the way home from work, weren't you?" She opens the front door, reaches inside and retrieves from the ashtray a still warm pipe.

"I'll be darned," dad says. "It was so warm out, I drove home with the windows down. And the wind must have..."

"And you wanted to blame poor Dennis Brandy! If it weren't for Dennis your whole car might have been in flames by now."

"Now, Betty, all's well that ends well. On Saturday I'll get some new seatcovers. I actually needed new ones anyway, so in a way this is a good thing."

"And if your car had burned to the ground would you be saying, 'well, we needed a new one anyway?' I'm just furious."

"Now, Betty, let's go eat. I'm starved. Come on kids." He reaches into his pocket and pulls out a quarter. "Here, Dennis. This is for saving my car. I knew you didn't start that fire."

Tommy looks at Linda. "Can you believe it? If it weren't for Dennis that ugly Nash would have burned to the ground and we could have bought a real car."

"Real car? You've got to be kidding. That's what we thought when the ugly "tub" got totaled."

Even though dad moved us far from his family, he remained very close to them. One Sunday a month, we would drive to the north side of Chicago to spend the day with his family. We would go to Aunt Mary's house and all of his other sisters and brothers and their families would come over.

Now before we would get to Aunt Mary's, we would stop for lunch. Dad knew that when we got to his sisters we would not eat for a long time and he didn't want us to arrive hungry, so he would always stop at a place called Art's Pizza — never, not even once, did we go anywhere but Art's Pizza. Now I'm not complaining, but looking back, wouldn't you think just once we might have tried a different place? That would not be *routine*! And once inside and we were seated, dad would order four Italian sausage sandwiches and four Pepsi's. We never had pizza, not even once. There were probably other wonderful things on the menu, but sausage sandwiches it was. They were delicious but I still would have loved to try the pizza!

Arriving at Mary's, quite full from our sausage sandwiches, the grownups would usually congregate in the kitchen, while the kids were delegated to a room off the kitchen. This, of course, was during winter months. In the summer, we all sat outside on their patio. We had lots of cousins to play with and we always had a good time. But the thing we all looked forward to most was supper. Aunt Mary was the best cook in the world. Our favorite meal was her specialty — homemade ravioli. She and my Aunt Ada would spend hours rolling out the dough on the kitchen table, filling it with wonderful cheeses, then rolling out the top dough. Then they would be cut into squares, several hundred of them. Some would be put in the freezer for later use. The rest would be cooked for dinner that day. It seemed like a lot of work but it was the best ravioli I have ever had. When we'd arrive, a large pot of spaghetti sauce would be cooking on the stove, filling the air with a wonderful aroma. Late in the day, everyone would gather around the big kitchen table and feast on this wonderful food. Aunt Mary also made wonderful desserts, and after everyone was finished with supper, Tommy and I would eagerly wait to see what kind of dessert she had made. My favorites were the wonderful Italian cookies she baked. The best part was that she would always give mom a box of them to take home with us.

We are in the breakfast nook, seated around the table for supper. Mom has made a round steak, mashed potatoes, peas, and a big salad. The salad won't be brought to the table until after we've cleaned our plates. There is also a bottle of wine on

the table, but no wine glasses. Dad drank his home made concord grape wine out of a small juice glass. Mom sometimes took a few sips, and grandma sometimes drizzled a few drops of wine in her chicken soup, turning it a curious color.

Dad starts cutting into the big flat steak and slides the first piece onto his own plate. His piece contains the round bone that he loves to suck on long after the meat has disappeared. Linda and Tommy wish there were more than one bone in a round steak. They think it's a little unfair that dad always gets the bone. But... bones apparently are for adults only.

Dad is in a bad mood. His older brother Bill is back in the hospital. Poor Uncle Bill. Last year he went into the hospital for a routine operation on his foot, a bone spur on his heel, and when he came out of the anesthesia he was completely paralyzed on one side of his body. This morning Aunt Mary, dad's sister, had called mom to tell her Uncle Bill hadn't been feeling well, and now he was back in the hospital.

Aggravating dad's mood is the fact that on the way home from work he got a traffic ticket.

"Were you speeding?" mom asks.

"No, I wasn't speeding. The cop said I made an ill-conceived left hand turn. Have you ever heard of such a thing?" We all looked at each other, including grandma. No, none of us had heard of such a thing.

"I think he made it up," Tommy said. "He needed to make his ticket quota for the day, dad."

Dad repeats the words: "Ill-conceived left hand turn. Who the hell ever heard of such a thing?"

"How much will it cost?" mom asks.

"Twenty-five bucks," dad says. "That's almost a day's wages. It really burns my ass."

Tommy starts to laugh, because sometimes dad tells a corny joke that goes: "You know what burns my ass? A flame about this high," at which point he takes one hand and holds it just below his butt.

Dad says, "I can't wait to tell Lee." He owns Lee's Gas Station in Tinley Park, a town about five miles away. Dad has been taking his cars to Lee for as long as the kids can remember. Dad holds Lee in the highest regard. He trusts Lee. He respects Lee. Lee's opinion on anything having to do with cars is gospel for our dad. Recently, he had even started buying his tires at Lee's, even though Lee's tires were a little more expensive than at the Goldblatt's in Markham.

"What can Lee do about your ticket, dad?" Linda asks.

Dad is busy chewing and doesn't answer.

"Linda asked you a question, Tom," mom says.

Dad refills his plate with more mashed potatoes, and takes a long sip of his wine. He continues to chew as he saws off a slice of the Gonnella Italian loaf.

"I just want to know if Lee has ever heard of an ill-conceived left hand turn," dad says. "If there is such a thing, Lee will have heard of it. If he hasn't heard of it, then this cop just made it up."

"How's the steak?" mom asks.

"Delicious," Tommy says. "Of course, some of us don't have a bone..."

"Tommy, your father works very hard all day...don't begrudge him that bone. You know he loves it."

"Yeah," Linda says. "Dad deserves it, you don't."

"You deserve a good smack," Tommy tells her.

Grandma says, "No, Tommy. Don't be mean to your sister."

"He's always mean to me, grandma. He was born mean."

"Can I have some salad now, mom?"

Mom gets up and walks to the kitchen counter where there is a big bowl of dandelion salad. The dandelions are fresh from grandma's morning walk, where she filled a shopping bag along Crawford Avenue. It took her more than four hours to fill that shopping bag, then another hour to wash the dandelions. Now, with the vinegar and oil dressing and a hardboiled egg thrown in for good measure, a salad doesn't get any better than this. The family will wipe up that bowl with the Gonnella bread so clean it wouldn't need washing.

Grandma says, "These dandelions would have been better last week. I should have picked them a week ago."

Mom clears her throat. "Tommy, are you going to tell dad about Linda's bike?"

"What about Linda's bike?" dad asks. He's sucking loudly on that round steak bone.

"Mom, not now," Tommy says.

"What about Linda's bike?" dad asks again. He picks up the wine bottle and refills his glass.

"Jerry lost it," Linda pipes up. Linda feels the weight of Tommy's foot on hers. He glares at her. Jerry is Tommy's best friend. Jerry lives with his deaf mother and his crazy older brother. He plays tricks on his deaf mother, such as turning off the vacuum sweeper when she's not looking. "Jerry!" his mother yells. "This sweeper's not picking up the dirt. Something's wrong with it." So Jerry walks over and flips the switch. "Okay, I fixed it, mom."

"Jerry didn't lose it," Tommy says. "His brother sold it."

Dad puts down his bone. "Jerry's brother sold Linda's bike? You said his brother sold YOUR bike last month. How the hell did Jerry's brother get Linda's bike?"

Mom says, "Tommy loaned it to Jerry the other day because he didn't have a way to get home."

Dad says, "So, let me get this straight. A few weeks ago he borrowed Tommy's bike and Jerry's brother sold it. So then you let Jerry borrow Linda's bike and now you're telling me his brother sold it too."

Linda thinks: It was a rusty old bike. Now maybe I can get a new one, like Kerry has.

No one at the table says a word. Dad says, "Remind me never to loan Jerry the car."

Everyone laughs, and Tommy says, "Dad, please let Jerry borrow the Nash. Please!" Now Linda agrees. "Yeah dad, let

Jerry borrow the Nash. Right now!" The kids crack up with laughter.

Tommy tries to picture what Jerry is doing at just this moment. He pictures Jerry arguing with his older, crazy brother, who doesn't work.

"You can laugh all you want, but just ask Lee what he thinks about that car. Lee says the Nash Ambassador is right up there with the Cadillac, at half the price. Lee says that hydramatic transmission in the Nash is the best on the road. He ought to know."

Mom says, "Last Saturday when Lee called to say your car was ready, he was very nice on the phone. I believe him."

Dad says, "I was telling Petrikas about Lee at the office today." Johnny Petrikas is dad's boss. Dad makes $5000 a year and Johnny Petrikas makes $8000. Just imagine what another $3000 a year could do! Dad continues, "Johnny has been having problems with his Buick and I told him to take it to Lee's."

"But Johnny lives an hour away from Lee's garage," mom says.

Dad helps himself to the bottom of the salad bowl. "This is the best part," he says, not for the first time.

The kitchen is a bright yellow and the late evening sun shines in. There are flowered curtains on the kitchen windows. Outside, someone at the Brandy house is trying to start their new power mower. Tommy and Linda have been on a campaign to get dad to buy one.

"Grandma could mow our yard twice as fast if she had a power mower, couldn't you grandma?"

Grandma shakes her head. "Too loud," she says.

"You could wear earmuffs," Linda says, cheerfully.

Dad says, "Well, ask your mother to start saving for it."

"Oh, sure, and how much do I have to save? Don't forget, I'm already saving for a new washing machine and a new toaster. And what about the tape recorder you want like Uncle Charleys?"

"A toaster?" Tommy says. "You have to save to buy a toaster? Good grief, it's not like they're a thousand dollars or anything?"

Dad cuts in: "Walker says he heard that power mowers are over rated. He says he'd never waste money on one." Walker's house is just down the street, on the other side of the Brandy house.

"Dad," Linda says. "Walker's yard is so small, you could fit 10 of them in our yard. He could cut his yard with a pair of scissors."

"He hardly ever mows it," Tommy says. "It's mostly weeds."

Mom says, "The inside of their house isn't much better. Bonnie is very nice but she doesn't know how to clean."

"Well, Betty, no one can clean like you," dad says.

The Walkers are a strange family, but Tommy and Linda like going over there occasionally because Mr. Walker is a welder and he raises foxes. Sometimes, late at night, you could see the *bright blue flame from Mr. Walker's welding torch a block away. Why Walker raised foxes is something they never thought to ask. He was simply a neighbor who welded and raised foxes. The Walkers, Bonnie and George, had a plump daughter named Donna who was a few years older than Tommy and Linda. Donna thought there was nothing unusual about having a father who welded and fed foxes into the night. But because Tommy and Linda's dad had a nine to five office job, Mr. Walker seemed interesting, if odd. Also, Mr. Walker always looked as if he hadn't shaved for a week, and his face was always red. It was red when he arrived on Friday night for his drinking sessions with dad, and it was redder still when he left two hours later. Despite the fact that the Walker house was only a hundred yards away, George Walker always drove over in his beat up pick up truck. Once, about a year earlier, Walker had backed out of our driveway and promptly ended up in the muddy ditch. "Well, I guess I'll just leave it here tonight," Walker said sadly. "I guess I'll have to walk home," and he stared down the road in the direction of his house as if it were miles away. For a moment Linda thought mom would offer to drive him home. Walker's name didn't suit him at all.*

Mom stands up, goes to the stove and brings the big yellow glass coffee pot to the table. "Do you want a cup, Ma?" she asks grandma. Mom asks grandma this question every night, and grandma's answer is always the same.

"Just a half cup," grandma says.

"What's for dessert?" Linda asks.

"What makes you think there's dessert?" mom asks. But then she smiles and we know that she baked something. She walks to the cupboard and returns with a chocolate cake.

"Now this makes me very happy," Linda says.

"Happy as a clam," Tommy says.

"How do you know clams are happy?" Linda asks.

Dad says, "This guy I work with, his wife is named Gladys. Nobody likes her because she puts on airs. Anyway, we all refer to her as happybottom." He laughs and looks around the table.

"Happy bottom?" Linda says.

Tommy laughs, "Glad-ass... happy bottom. Get it?"

Linda suddenly gets it and laughs hysterically, repeating the words over and over. Glad-ass, happybottom, Glad-ass, happybottom.

Mom says, "You certainly don't call her that name in front of her husband, do you?"

"Well, Betty, one of the guys accidentally asked him one day how happybottom was, and he thought it was so funny he now calls her happybottom himself...though not to her face, of course."

"Some day he'll slip," Tommy says.

The phone rings. Linda, as usual, jumps up and grabs it. "Hello?" she says loudly, with a mouthful of cake.

She looks at dad. "Yes, we're just finishing, Aunt Mary. I'll put him on." She hands the receiver to dad.

"Hi Mary," dad says. "Are you calling about Bill? Have

you heard anything yet?"

There is a silence for a few moments. Then dad stands up from the table. He shares a few more words with his sister and then hangs up.

"Bill is gone," dad says. We all look at him, at his face. Dad looks at his wrist watch. "He died at 5:33, just 10 minutes ago." He turns and walks out of the kitchen and goes to his bedroom. Mom goes in to comfort him, but dad doesn't come out for the rest of the night.

We had spent our supper time talking about the things families talk about: a traffic ticket, a missing bike, dandelions, saving money to buy things like power mowers and washing machines, and a neighbor who raises foxes. And while we had been talking about these things, Uncle Bill was dying. If we had known he was dying we would probably have talked about something else, something more important, more serious. But it was too late for that now, so Tommy and Linda got up from the table and went outside to play. It was a beautiful spring evening.

Dad had a really great sense of humor and loved telling jokes and doing magic tricks. Everyone who knew him said he was the funniest person they knew. He would tell the silliest jokes over and over and we would laugh over and over. He loved to do coin tricks and when he did them he would always say "the hand is quicker than the eye," and we never tired of hearing him say it.

He loved to pull a coin out from behind someone's ear or make coins disappear and he really was very good at it. The same with a deck of cards. He was very good at doing card tricks, and any time we had a crowd, he'd be sure to do a few for them, especially the younger kids. They, of course, would ooh and ah.

He was not a romantic person, nor a sentimental one, but you knew he cared deeply about his family. I don't know if he and mom ever had a really deep passion between them because I never saw them kiss, hug, hold hands, or show any outward signs of affection, other than one time when I saw him put his arm around her. I do know the marriage worked because they had a genuine respect, trust, and admiration for each other. Then again, who knows, maybe they did have that passion, but kept it private between them. I know mom thought he was the greatest guy that ever lived. Tommy and I seldom heard them fight or have harsh words with one another. Their fights consisted of mom getting annoyed at something he did, like maybe having a beer too many. She'd complain, and in typical dad fashion, he'd just sort of roll his eyes, look at us kids, and say with a half smile, "Your mom's mad at me." Then he'd proceed to humor her a bit, and next thing you knew, our house was back to normal and mom was back to cleaning the house she loved so much, for the man she loved so much. He rarely yelled at, or disciplined, Tommy and me. He left all of that up to mom. That was just his nature. Very laid back, he didn't let too much get to him. He took life pretty much in stride and saw good in most people. Criticism was not a part of his make up, and he didn't like hearing gossip either. He was tolerant of most people and wanted Tommy and me to be like that, too.

For two weeks each year, dad would break from the routine. That was when he would get two weeks vacation. His company closed down the first two weeks in August every year, and while we never took a vacation as a family away from the house, we used the two weeks to do things that weren't part of the normal routine. And they were just about the best two weeks of the year. Tommy and I looked forward all year just for those two weeks. And even though it broke from the daily routine, the two weeks vacation itself was very routine every year.

Without exception, during that two week period we would always attend a White Sox baseball game. Being "south siders," we were huge Sox fans. We had the best time sitting in the bleachers, eating hot dogs, peanuts, and anything else we wanted. That was one day when they were pretty generous in letting us eat a lot of "junk." It didn't matter whether or not the Sox won, at least not to me. Tommy would say otherwise, I'm sure. For me, it was just fun to be out at the park with my family. Another thing we always did was go to Riverview Park. Anyone over the age of 50 reading this who lived in the Midwest has probably heard of Riverview. It was the greatest amusement park in the area. We would usually go on either 2 cent day or 5 cent day and we would stay until the park closed late at night. And what a time we had. The lines were very short, especially in comparison to the lines at today's theme parks. And after the ride was over, you could just hand the attendant more money and stay on the ride. You could keep doing this all day. They didn't care. If you had money, you could stay on and ride. And what rides they had: The Bobs…the greatest roller coaster in its day; Aladdin's Castle, greatest fun house in the world; The Pair-o-chutes, the only one of its kind at that time. Flying Turns, Silver Flash, Blue Streak, House of Hades, Shoot the Chutes, and the Rotor, were also some of my favorites. Oh, the fun we had, and the memories we still have. The day and night would pass by so quickly. We didn't want it to end because we knew it would be another year before we would go there again.

We had a racetrack in a neighboring town, and because dad loved to play the horses, during the two week vacation, he would forgo placing a bet at the Long Bar on Saturday mornings. Instead, he would go out to Washington Park almost every day for a few hours, unless it was a day when we were going some where else. Once or twice during each vacation, he would let Tommy and me come with him.

One Saturday morning in August, 1955, our family woke up to a beautiful day. Dad had been on vacation all week, he had one more week to go, and today he was taking Tommy and Linda to the race track—Washington Park Race Track. Washington Park was only about five miles from our house, and it was

considered a world class thoroughbred track, attracting the best horses and the best jockeys from around the world.

Tommy was particularly excited that morning, because tonight he would be going out on one of his first real dates — a boy/girl party, with a girl named Dianne (two n's please) from nearby Tinley Park. He and mom had already gone shopping earlier in the week for a new sports jacket and dress shirt — but suddenly that morning he realized he had forgot all about a new tie.

Dad came to the rescue. "Here, Tommy," he said, "pick out one of my ties." In his closet there were about a hundred of the fattest, widest, old-fashioned ties you could imagine. Many of them had Hawaiian themes with lots of palm trees. "Pick one, and I'll show you how to tie the best Windsor Knot on the block." This was a large knot that was difficult to tie.

So Tommy picked out the only skinny tie on the rack and dad set about teaching him the intricacies of the Windsor Knot. Before Tommy could perfect it, it was time to get to the track. Post time for the first of the eight races was at 1:00.

In the car, we could see the huge grandstand of the Washington Park Race Track from more than a mile away. As we got closer, the traffic got thicker, until cars were reduced to a crawl during the final few blocks entering the enormous parking lot. The closer we got, the more exciting everything became. When we had parked our car, the three of us started walking briskly — then running — to the ticket windows. Hundreds, thousands of people, ran alongside. It's not that we were late for *anything; rather, we were all just caught up in the excitement of it all.*

At the ticket window, dad made it clear to the seller that Tommy and I were "under 12"—meaning we got in for free. (The fact that Tommy was actually 14 bothered me a little—did dad just forget Tommy's real age, or was he fibbing so as to avoid having to pay for a ticket?)

Once inside, there were arrows pointing toward grandstand seats and the box seats in the Clubhouse. Dad headed us in the direction of the grandstand seats. "We actually have a better view of the race from where we will be seating," dad announced. (Why, I wondered, did the box seats cost more, if that was the case?)

I will never forget the sight of that race track when you first walk through the ramps and get a view of this one mile oval, surrounded by rich shrubbery and flowers and the greenest grass, as far as the eye could see. It was perfectly manicured, every inch of it, and there, in front of the middle of the grandstand, stood the totalizator board—or tote board—lit up with hundreds of numbers showing the odds, weights, entry numbers, and a dozen other digits that only a professional gambler would know. On the way in, dad bought the Daily Racing Form and the Red Sheet. Many racing fans also bought the Green Sheet, but dad was always loyal to the Red Sheet because once, about 10 years earlier, this tip sheet picked a 20–1 longshot that won and netted dad a cool $40.00.

When we were seated, dad settled into an analysis of the day's races, and Tommy and I headed down to the paddocks. We loved to watch the horses up close, as their trainers saddled them, and walked them in small circles, and we especially liked when the jockeys, in their beautifully bright colored silks, strode purposefully, single-file, from their dressing rooms into the paddock stalls. They looked like little boys with grown men's faces, and they seemed to avoid eye-contact as they walked straight to their mount, and allowed the trainers to help hoist them up. Then we ran from the paddock area out to the rail of the track to watch the horses' post parade.

We enjoyed trying to help dad pick the winner of each race. He taught us how to read the racing form: weight, age, class, jockey, track conditions, past performances—all had to be figured into the equation. Dad refused to bet on the favorites— they didn't pay enough to make it interesting, and since they only won 30 percent of the time, why not try to pick the horse most likely to beat the favorite. This was always dad's mission.

He always came to the track with $25. This covered admission, a minimum $2.00 bet on each race ($16.00), and enough left over to buy some hot dogs and drinks. It was a rare Saturday that we left the track with much money left over.

There were eight races on the card, a half hour between races. And there wasn't a dull minute in the entire four hours. Tommy and I spent a lot of time looking for lost winning tickets. By the third or fourth race, the ground was covered with the colorful tickets—thousands and thousands of tickets that had been purchased with great hope and then discarded with disgust. And within an hour after arriving, we each had a huge stack of these tickets, and between races we examined each one, hoping against hope that some poor jerk had thrown away a winner. Dad had once told us that he knew someone, who knew someone, who knew someone, who had once found a winning ticket. Someone else he knew, knew someone who had thrown away a winning ticket by mistake. The fact that we never found such a winner never seemed to discourage us.

On this particular Saturday, seven races had been run, the hot dogs eaten, the money almost gone—and dad had yet to make a single trip to the cashiers windows (that's where you redeemed winning tickets). Not one of his horses had even been "in the money" (finished 1st 2nd or 3rd). And now dad was studying the entries for the eighth race, and as he had often done in the past, he decided he needed to play a true long-shot if he wanted to come out ahead for the day.

"Come on, kids, help me try to find a good long shot," dad said, as we returned from yet one more trip to the paddock. Tommy picked up the Red Sheet, looked at the names of the horses in the race, and one of them suddenly jumped off the page. It was horse number 12, named Wins or Not. "Dad," he exclaimed. "Look at number 12, his name is Wins or Not. Isn't this a coincidence? You showed me how to tie a Windsor Knot just this morning! Let's bet on him."

Dad had kind of made up his mind on another horse, but he consulted the racing form and studied Wins or Not's past performances. "There's a reason he's 50–1," dad said. "He hasn't placed in the money all year long, he's moving up in class, and he doesn't like the turf course. Besides, his jockey is having a bad year."

"But dad, please..."

"Sorry, kids, this nag doesn't have a chance. We'd be wasting our money."

The horses broke from the starting gate, and two minutes later, Wins or Not, after starting dead last, charged down the home stretch and won the race by a nose in a photo finish. Tommy and I were speechless. On a $2.00 bet, the horse paid $102. Oh, why hadn't dad gone along with our hunch! We just knew this horse was going to win.

As Tommy and I trudged toward the exit doors in a cloud of gloom, dad waited until the last minute to spring his surprise. He pulled two tickets from his shirt pocket. One of them was the horse he favored, which had finished "out of the money." The other one was number 12 — Wins or Not. "As I was placing my bet," dad said, "I couldn't help thinking about the tie and the horse. And though I always bet on only one horse per race, I figured I'd make an exception this time. Sure glad I did. Let's go collect, kids."

Tommy and I each still had a fistful of losing tickets we had been collecting, and we stared at the winning ticket in awe. This *was a winning ticket! This is what a winning ticket looked like. And we all walked together to the cashier's window and watched as dad slid the ticket under the glass and watched the cashier count out $102. It looked like a huge amount of money.*

That evening when Tommy dressed to go out on his date, he spent a half hour perfecting the Windsor Knot on his tie. Now, 50 years later, he no longer thinks about the girl with two n's in her name, but every single time he puts on a tie, he recalls that day, that horse—and his dad.

The rest of his two week vacation was spent around the house. Dad would take care of a lot of little things mom wanted done. He also had more time to spend with us. He would come outside and play baseball, or shoot basketballs. He and Tommy would go to the driving range and hit a bucket or two of balls. Next to the driving range was a miniature golf course, and now and then he'd bring mom and me with, and after shooting their bucket of balls, we'd all play a round of miniature golf. Afterwards, we'd stop at the nearby Tastee Freeze and get a frozen custard. We'd go to bed happy that night.

One of dad's outside enjoyments was joining the Loyal Order of Moose. He became quite active, joining both the Ritual Team and the Drill Team. He traveled extensively with the Moose, entering competitions in various cities. He would wear a uniform for the Drill Team and a tuxedo for the Ritual Team, and while

I'd only get to see pictures, he looked pretty neat. There were family activities as well. Once a year they held an annual picnic which we would always attend. There was always plenty of food and lots of games for kids. Throughout the year they also had children's parties for special occasions like Christmas, Easter and Halloween.

My favorite, though, was going to Mooseheart, a self-contained city in Batavia, Illinois, about 1-1/2 hours from our home. It was open to children of Moose members from all over the United States who had lost one or both of their parents. They had their own schools, shops, and churches. In some instances, if only the father was gone, the mother could come and live at Mooseheart, too. That didn't mean she could live in the same room with her kids. She couldn't. All the kids slept in dorms according to age. But the mothers could live on the grounds and usually they got jobs working at the school, in the stores, or any other positions available. At least they were near their children. Once a year they opened the place for visitors. Moose members from all over the United States would come to spend a day there. They called it Mooseheart Day. We could go through all the dorms and see where the kids lived, visit their schools and shops, and towards the end of the day, they held a huge parade and all the kids living there would put on some type of program at the football stadium. I always felt bad when we'd go there, knowing all these children had lost either one or both of their parents. But then dad, in his ultimate wisdom, would point out to me that, while they may not have parents, they did have a wonderful place to live, with people who cared about them. They were receiving a good education, and he'd remind me that there were many orphaned children all over the world who did not have such a place to live. That would make me feel somewhat better.

Our property had lots of trees, both shade and fruit. We had several apple trees, a peach tree, a plum tree, and one huge cherry tree that, for some reason, produced the most sour cherries that were always full of worms. We also had several rows of grape vines that grew the sweetest and tastiest grapes in the world, the concord grape. In October when they were at their ripest, I couldn't get enough of them. I'd grab a bunch every chance I could. Mom would put them in our school lunches, which was always a treat. She would make grape jelly, too, enough to last until the next season's grapes were ready. Dad loved the grape vineyard, too, but for slightly different reasons. I was probably around five or six the first time I remember dad making wine, Dago Red he called it. He bought a used wine press, two huge wooden barrels, and where he got the recipe to make the wine I have no idea, but in the garage that one October and for many years thereafter, it became a fall event. Dad would spend hours in the garage pressing the grapes and doing whatever else that needed to be done to make wine.

Since our own vineyard didn't produce enough grapes, Mr. Walker would drive dad in his pickup to Michigan where he would buy more grapes, as many bushels that would fit into the back of the pickup. That first season, when dad finished making the wine, he covered up the barrel with a large, heavy canvas, and there it would stay fermenting for the next 14 months. Dad said he would tap it the following Christmas. Tommy and I wanted to know why it would take so long, and Dad explained the fermenting process to us, saying if he tapped it too soon, the wine wouldn't be any good. The next 14 months probably seemed like an eternity to Dad.

The following October, once again he went through the process of making wine, and when finished, he put it in the second barrel, covered it with another canvas and let that barrel begin its 14 month fermenting process. "Dad," Tommy asked, "you don't even know if the first barrel is any good. Aren't you taking a chance making a second barrel?"

"Tommy," dad said, "if I don't make a second barrel now, then the following year I won't have any wine. Life is all about chances, and I'm willing to take that chance. We'll know in just two more months."

Christmas morning, when everyone else was probably opening up their presents, dad, mom, Tommy and I went out to the garage. The moment he had been waiting for finally arrived. Dad carefully removed the canvas from the first barrel, and then quite ceremoniously, held the wine decanter under the tap. As the wine began to fill the decanter, dad said, "Well, it sure looks like wine." When the bottle was full, he held it up to his nose, took a deep breath, and exclaimed that it smelled like wine. We all followed him into the house. Dad got a small glass and poured a little wine into it. We all waited while he took that first sip. Suddenly a broad grin crossed his face, and he proudly boasted, "It tastes like wine. It's delicious." We were all so excited for him. He then poured a little for mom and for grandma, who had just come downstairs. They tasted it and then he said Tommy and I could have a little sip, too.

All our neighbors knew about the wine and were anxious to try some. That day, and for many Christmas mornings to come, Dad would make the rounds to all the neighbors, bringing each of them a bottle of wine. They looked forward to his Christmas visit, and they would all insist he have a small glass with them to toast the holiday season and, of course, to pay homage to the newly tapped barrel of wine. "Just a sip," he would say. "Betty will raise the roof if I come home tipsy." So a quick sip (or two) and off he'd go to the next neighbor where it would start all over again. By the time he'd get back home, he surely would have had one sip too many, but it was Christmas, and this one time each year, mom wouldn't get mad at him. She'd just give him a knowing smile and suggest that maybe he'd like to take a short nap before company arrived. And he would. She'd send Tommy and me upstairs to play so as not to make too much noise while he slept.

Besides having great fruit trees, we also had some huge poplars. One tree in particular was the best climbing tree in the world. Tommy and I spent endless summer days playing in that tree. To this day, we refer to it as "our tree." We would climb up to our favorite branch and then jump down. This was especially fun to do in the fall. We'd rake all the leaves, and there were tons, into a huge pile under the tree, then jump. One time I was climbing up the tree and he was right behind me. When I got to our usual branch, he suggested I climb higher. So like a good sport, I climbed to the next highest branch I could safely get to. Next thing I knew Tommy was below me hollering for me to go up even one more branch. "No, I can't. You know this is as high as I can climb," I cried. "Well, I'm coming up to the branch you are on. If you don't go one higher, the branch will break from the weight of both of us. Here I come!" Believing he would actually do it, I frantically struggled to climb to the next branch. I had never been that high before and I was a little scared. When I got safely to that next branch, once again he threatened to climb up to the branch I was on, and he said he would keep on climbing till I reached the top of the tree. I was so scared that I started climbing my little heart out. I climbed higher and higher till I was at the top of this giant tree. When I caught my breath, I looked down to see how close behind me he was. He wasn't there. And though the tree branches were very dense, I knew he wasn't in the tree any more. All the while I'm climbing higher, he was climbing back down. I just sat in that tree frozen, unable to move. I started shouting for mom. She came out and, while crying, I tried to tell her what happened. Tommy, as usual, wormed his way out of it. "But, mom, honestly, I didn't do it on purpose. I was climbing and suddenly I had to go really bad, so

I climbed back down to go to the bathroom. I didn't know she'd keep climbing. It's not my fault." She not only bought his ridiculous story, but proceeded to get rather upset with me because I couldn't climb down by myself and she had to climb the tree and help me down.

From Tommy's bedroom, we could climb out onto the roof of the house and run up and down from one side of the house to another. Sometimes Tommy would jump from the house onto the garage roof, which was lower than the house roof, and from the garage roof he'd jump to the ground. He always pleaded with me to jump with him, but I was too afraid. I knew I could probably jump onto the garage roof, but jumping all the way to the ground was something else. I was sure I couldn't do that without breaking my leg. Mom had warned us repeatedly not to go out on the roof. It was quite steep and she was certain we'd fall and get hurt. It was definitely off limits. One afternoon mom said she was going down to the end of the block to visit Mrs. Walker. As soon as she left, Tommy and I went up to his room and climbed out onto the roof. We ran up and down all over and had lots of fun. Then Tommy jumped onto the garage roof. "Come on, Linda, jump. You can make it." "I know I can, but you know I can't jump to the ground," I said. "And I certainly can't jump back *up* to the house roof to climb back in through the window." "Don't worry, I've got that all figured out. Here's what we'll do. Jump down to the garage roof. We'll play for a while and when we're ready to get down, I'll jump down to the ground and get a ladder to put against the garage. You can climb down from there. Mom will never know. It will be fun." So since it did sound like fun, and I really was dying to get on the garage roof, I jumped. It was quite easy to do and we did have fun. After about 10 minutes we thought we better not press our luck on having mom come back and find us on the roof. "We better get down now," I said. "Okay, wait here. I'll be back with a ladder in a few minutes." Tommy jumped down while I waited for a ladder. I waited and waited, and no ladder. After so many of Tommy's tricks, it didn't take a genius to realize a ladder wasn't coming. I started hollering as loud as I could. There was nothing I could do but sit there. It seemed like forever before I saw mom coming down the road. I wasn't sure if I was glad to see her or not. She saw me immediately sitting on the roof and was really angry. All the while she was putting up a ladder for me to climb down, she was yelling. I tried to tell her what happened but Tommy had his own version. He said, "Mom, I'm sorry. I admit we did go out on the roof even though you told us not to, but I begged Linda not to jump to the garage. Honestly — she just wouldn't listen. I was just getting ready to come down to Walkers and get you so you could help her get down. I was so worried about her." Mom thought that was the sweetest thing.

The floors in that old house creaked, the lighting was poor, and, as I mentioned earlier, there were no doors on the bedrooms. I was always just a little fearful to go upstairs by myself at night because it was so dark and I never knew what Tommy was up to.

Mom would usually come upstairs with me until I turned on my bedroom light. One such evening, after mom had come upstairs with me, we talked for a few minutes and then she went downstairs. I got into my jams, turned out the light and climbed into bed. A few minutes later as I was lying there, I began to feel a sort of lump in my mattress. It would push up and then slowly go back down. It kept happening and I kept getting more scared with each lump I felt. Finally, I shrieked, "MOMMMMM, come quick." She came running up the stairs into my room. I told her what was happening to my bed and she said I was letting my imagination run away. She said she would sit with me a few minutes until I calmed down. We sat for a short time but nothing happened. "See, Linda, there's nothing strange going on. Now go to sleep." As she was getting ready to leave, dad came upstairs, peeked in my room and said, "Where's Tommy?" "In his room," mom said. "No, he isn't. I was just in there. And he isn't downstairs either." As if on cue, mom and I both jumped off the bed and looked underneath. And lo, there was Tommy, lying flat on the floor with his feet up in the air pressing against the mattress, trying to stifle a laugh. For once, mom finally believed me. She told him to get to his room and never, ever to do that again. He promised he wouldn't, but for years afterward, I would always peek under my bed before getting into it.

The house had several attic closets. One of them you could access through a door in my bedroom. There were no lights in the attics so it was really dark in there, and ice cold in the winter and sweltering in the summer. Mom just stored a lot of junk in there. On another night, after I had gone to bed, but not before checking under the bed, I was almost asleep when I started to hear very soft moans, followed by a series of soft taps. They'd end quickly, and just when I was convinced I was imagining things, the moans would start all over again, very faint, followed by more tapping sounds. By now I was getting scared, and so once again I started calling for mom. She came running upstairs and I told her what was happening. Suddenly, I spotted something. I noticed the door to the attic was not completely closed. Bingo — I knew what the strange sounds were. Before mom could do any investigating, I quickly told her that I was sure it was only the wind and my vivid imagination playing tricks on me, and that she didn't have to stay with me. "Go on back downstairs," I said. "I'll be just fine." "Well, if you're sure. Okay. Goodnight." As soon as she left, I quickly slammed the attic door shut. I knew Tommy was in there. Many times dad had said that he had to put a doorknob inside the attic doors so no one could ever accidentally get locked in there, but I knew he had never gotten around to doing it. Tommy was literally trapped in there. Revenge, at last! He started begging me to let him out, but I wouldn't. I told him I was going to make up for all the mean things he did to me. And then I said, loud enough for him to hear me, "I think I'll go downstairs and get something to eat. There's one piece of apple pie left." And I turned out my bedroom light and happily marched downstairs. Now I'd like to say that I won that round, but actually I didn't, not quite. Tommy started pounding loud and hollering. Mom and dad both heard it and went running upstairs. There they found Tommy in the attic, frantic, although I knew he was hamming it up for their sake. Needless to say, he milked it for everything he could. "Mom, dad, she locked me in the attic and wouldn't let me out. I could have suffocated, maybe even died. It must be 110 in here. I almost fainted." He did look all hot and exhausted. I then got yelled at for what I did, but, hallelujah, he in turn got yelled at for playing yet another trick on me. I guess it was a tie that night.

I Remember Mama

My mom was named Elizabeth Rose. Called Betty, she was the third of four daughters born to Leonardo and Mary Molin. Mom was a homemaker, if there ever was one. It's what she enjoyed. Caring for my dad, Tommy and me was her job in life, and she did it eagerly and happily. We had the cleanest house of any one I knew, Tommy and I had the cleanest and neatest clothes, the shiniest shoes; she even kept our gym shoes spotless with white shoe polish. My dad's white shirts were always starched and ironed to perfection, his suits and ties dry cleaned often. Our house had lots of windows, and they, too, were cleaner than anyone else's. At least once a month she would wash them all, inside and out, except in winter of course, and believe me, by spring time, the first warm day she would be out there washing them.

Like everything else in our home, many things were in major need of repair or replacement. Our kitchen and dining room floors were no exception. Mom and dad decided to put new tile down, and a bigger production you never saw in your life. Honestly, it took dad longer to decide on a floor pattern than to actually lay the tile. They chose a vinyl tile in two different colors, cream and a sort of a pale, faded red. Every night after supper, and after a half hour at the piano, dad would get out the tiles and place them on the floor, and there he would spend the next hour or so configuring patterns. When he liked one, mom wouldn't, and vice versa. Now and then he'd ask Tommy and me which pattern we liked, but I think he was only being polite. I don't think he really cared because he certainly wasn't going to choose something we liked that maybe he didn't. This was his project and he was really into it. Now this might be hard to imagine in your head, but the pattern he finally decided on made sort of an "L" design, with the "L" being the red tiles, and turned in different directions. All the rest were the cream tiles. We really thought it was beautiful when it was finished and so did dad. Mom, of course, was in heaven with her new floors. For Christmas that year, along with the two pound box of chocolates he gave her every year, dad got her a combination floor scrubber/polisher/buffer. And lest you think she would have preferred perfume or jewelry, think again. A better gift he couldn't have given her. Every time I turned around, there she was buffing those floors. And even though she liked everything clean and shiny, it doesn't mean for a minute that our house wasn't lived in — quite the contrary. For instance, when Tommy and I got roller skates one year for Christmas, all winter long we would skate on the dining room floor. We'd get terrible scuff marks on the floor, but mom didn't mind. That night when we were finished skating, she'd get out the buffer and shine them to perfection again. And if we were in the mood to skate again the following night, that was okay with her. She knew how to get rid of those scuff marks very well.

Our dining room was quite large and we had a big table in it. One Christmas Tommy got a train set with a nice transformer and all sorts of tunnels and accessories to go with it. While it was fun to play with, it was a pain to keep putting it together then taking it apart. So dad went to the hardware store and bought a huge piece of thin plywood. He then assembled the train tracks by nailing them down. Now whenever Tommy wanted to play with the train, he would simply lay the plywood on the top of the dining room table, add the cars, and he was ready to go. Of course, the dining room got kind of messy because we had to take everything off the table, and push all the chairs out of the way. But again, mom didn't care. When we were through playing, dad and Tommy would carry the plywood out to the enclosed back porch. She would then painstakingly put everything back in its place.

Another thing all of us did together was play ping pong. We didn't have a ping pong table, and without a basement to put it in, dad didn't want to buy one. Instead, once again, he bought another large piece of thin plywood. Dad put the net on the plywood, then placed the plywood on top the dining room table.

Again we disheveled mom's dining room, and again she didn't care. When we were through playing, it would be stored on the back porch along with the train track plywood. Dad enjoyed playing ping pong, while mom just enjoyed watching all of us play. Dad and Tommy would play and then I'd play the winner, which was usually dad. When Tommy and I played together, at first he would always beat me, but then the more I kept playing I actually got very good at it. In fact, in 6th grade, I was the girls' champion at our school. I've always been quite proud of that feat, because as good as Tommy was, he did not become the boys' champion. All my practicing at home played off. That dining room table sure came in handy for lots of things besides eating. And mom never minded.

Mom baked at least twice a week. Midweek she would usually bake two pies, coconut cream (dad's favorite) and either lemon meringue or banana cream, or in the summer maybe a fresh peach or apple pie, and for special occasions, raisin pie. That was my favorite. On Fridays she would make a devil's food cake, from scratch. She would put creamy white frosting on it and top it with coconut (again, the dad thing). It was the moistest cake I've ever had. I can still recall how the house would smell on those days when we'd come home from school. She also would make what Tommy and I called "pie strips." After baking the pies, mom would take all the left over dough and roll it out. She would then cut the rolled dough into strips and bake them. Right out of the oven they were absolutely delicious. We enjoyed those pie strips as much as the pies.

In addition to the grape jelly mom made, she made plum jelly, too. Both were delicious, although grape was my favorite. She would put up enough jars to last the entire winter. She also took the apples and peaches that were left late in the season and put up jars of applesauce and canned peaches. It was a busy time in the kitchen in the fall. Not only did we have trees that produced wonderful fruits, but dad planted a huge garden. We would have fresh vegetables all summer to enjoy, and then in the fall she would spend days canning; and from the vegetable garden we would enjoy the likes of carrots, green beans, beets, stewed tomatoes and tomato juice all winter, too. It was hard work but that's what she loved to do.

Between keeping her home and family clean and well fed, she also found time to sew. She was an excellent seamstress and, as with everything else she did, she enjoyed it immensely. I owned very few store bought clothes, other than underwear and an occasional sweater, until I was a teenager. She not only made skirts, blouses, and dresses, she also made my pajamas and winter coats. We'd go to the fabric store together and she'd let me pick out some of the materials. I always looked forward to that. Besides making my clothes, there were added bonuses. She would make clothes for my dolls with the left over remnants. I had the best dressed dolls in town. And come Halloween, our costumes couldn't be beat. Every year in grade school, Tommy and I would win first prize in our respective classes. Over the years I was a southern belle, a gypsy, an Indian, and a hobo, to name a few. Never did we have a store-bought costume. Mom would have shuddered at such a thought. One year she made a Superman outfit for Tommy and you just wouldn't believe how authentic it looked. Tommy loved Superman at that time, so not only did he like it for Halloween, but long after he would continue to wear it. One day mom saw him on top the garage roof dressed in the Superman outfit. When she asked him what he was doing, he replied, "I'm going to fly." Now I'm not really sure if he would have tried, but mom wasn't about to take any chances. She ordered him down immediately. Our best costume, though, was the year she made Tommy and me matching cowboy/cowgirl outfits. They were made of the most beautiful brown material and she had put brown fringe down the sides of the arms and legs and across the chest and back. Complete with cowboy hats, boots, and 2-gun holsters, we not only took first place, but actually had our picture appear in the local paper. (In today's world, we would have had to leave the guns at home.) And our prize for winning first prize was the same every year — a taffy apple!

She was also a room mother for my class for many years. I loved having her as room mother and other kids loved having her, too, because she not only was nice, but she used to bring such good treats to all school parties. When I was about seven, I joined the brownies followed by girl scouts. They were in need of a scout leader so mom volunteered. During the week she would work on projects for the next meeting. We would meet once a week and everyone enjoyed having her as a scout leader. One time our troop was planning to visit a nursing home. We planned to sing songs for them and bring homemade cookies to pass around. Our troop started making the cookies the day before. We not only did a terrible job of baking, but the few good ones there were we ate as quickly as they came out of the oven. When the troop meeting was over and all the girls had been picked up by their parents, everyone was upset that we wouldn't have homemade cookies for the people when we visited them the next day. However, when we met at the nursing home the following day, mom arrived with a car load of cookies. She had stayed up long into the night baking them so the girls would have something to pass around, and she didn't mind at all. That's my mom!

Mom was a pretty woman, but she didn't seem to care all that much about how she looked. And I don't mean to imply that she looked a mess, because believe me, she didn't. It's just that she cared more about how Tommy, dad, and I looked. She rarely wore makeup, but when she did she looked beautiful. I used to love to watch her get dressed up because it was so seldom. The only times she would get dressed up was for some special occasion, or if she would go with dad to the Moose lodge on Saturday night for dancing. And when I'd see her all dressed up I'd think, "Why can't she always look like this." Around the house, though, she would wear house dresses that she had made, always clean and neatly ironed. Her hair was dark brown and naturally wavy, and I swear, she didn't appreciate it. I was always moaning that I got the poker straight hair, and Tommy got the wavy hair like mom. Oh, the injustice!

There was a wonderful hot dog stand not far from our home called Willies WeeNee Wagon. Their hot dogs and hamburgers were the best in the area and people from all over the neighboring towns came to Willies to eat. When Tommy was about 14, he applied for a job and Willie hired him. He was thrilled to have a job and make some spending money. Now and then his work schedule would have him come in early before they opened for business to get the place ready. This would entail cleaning the wagon, getting the steamers ready for the hot dogs, heating the grill, and slicing all the tomatoes and onions. Now, mom being mom, one Friday night Tommy had been out late, so Saturday morning she decided to let him sleep in. The wagon didn't open until 11:00, but he was supposed to go in to work at 8:00. Instead, mom went in and cleaned up the entire place spotless, of course. Then she sliced all the tomatoes and onions. By the time Tommy arrived, everything was done. All he had to do was start serving customers. Somehow, that started to become a ritual for them. Mom would go in early and let Tommy sleep. Willie started noticing how much cleaner the wagon had been looking lately, and one Saturday morning he showed up early. He was surprised to see mom there, but was also quite pleased at the job she was doing. He promptly offered her a permanent job, which she accepted. I can tell you it was the best decision Willie ever made, hiring my mom. She kept the place running to such perfection that I think even Willie was surprised. For 30 years she worked there and loved every minute of it. After work, she'd come home smelling of mustard and onions, just in time to make our supper and then take care of her own house. She never seemed to get tired — ever!

IT'S ALL RELATIVE

Grandma Mary (mom's mother) was born Maria Pais Becher in Auronzo, Italy, one of three children. She was raised by her father, her mother having died giving birth to her. When she was a young teen, she started seeing a boy named Leonardo Molin. Leonardo and his brother had an opportunity to come to America. They settled in St. Louis where an acquaintance from their village in Italy lived. Leonardo had promised grandma that once settled, he would send for her. Several years later, with the blessings of her father, she left Italy and came by boat to America, being sick every second she was at sea. It was not a pleasurable trip. Shortly after her arrival in the states, she and Leonardo married, and they moved to a small town in Illinois, just across the river from St. Louis, called Panama. He got a job working in the coal mines. Their first daughter Diane arrived, followed two years later by Delores, and two years after that my mom, Elizabeth, arrived. They would remain in Panama until the coal mines closed, probably around 1930. They moved to

Chicago where grandpa got a factory job. They would have one more daughter, Inez. There was a 10 year difference between my mom and baby Inez. The three older girls loved their new baby sister, but didn't like calling her Inez, so instead, they started calling her Honey. To this day, she is Aunt Honey to all of us. Grandpa died of a heart attack at a young age in 1945. The three older sisters were all married and on their own. Grandma and Aunt Honey continued to live in their apartment, but after a year or so, grandma was really strapped for money. Aunt Honey was nearing 18 when grandma sent her to live at our house.

Aunt Honey lived with us for a few years, and it was fun having her with us. I felt like she was my older sister. Over the next few years she would start dating. I would sit on her bed and watch her for hours on end fixing her hair and makeup to go out on a date. I thought it was so exciting. I'd get to meet the guys when they would come to pick her up, and then the next day I'd ask her all about it, where did they go, what did they do, and most important, did she like him. One man, in particular, I remember because he used to bring Tommy and me presents. One time he brought us both marionettes, Howdy Doody and Clarabelle. Another time he brought us hand puppets, The Lone Ranger and Hop-a-Long Cassidy, and still another time Tommy got the coolest holster, and I got the most beautiful doll I'd ever seen. We thought he was the nicest man in the world, but apparently Aunt Honey didn't think so, because after a few months, she quit going out with him. We never saw him again, and we never again got such nice gifts for no special occasion. We missed him.

Grandma Mary came to live with us when I was about seven years old, and it was one of the happier times of my life having her with us. I loved her so. She had one of the bedrooms upstairs, the only bedroom with a door. She spoke fairly good English but with a heavy Italian accent. Grandma was a hard worker and spent most of her time in the summer working in the large vegetable garden we had. She loved it. She'd be up on weekends at 6 a.m. just to get an early start with her hoeing and weeding. And in between, she'd mow the lawn, and believe me, there was lots of grass. The mower was an old fashioned kind with a rotary blade that you pushed manually. Years later dad would finally buy a power mower, but grandma never liked it and wouldn't use it. She preferred the old one. Another one of her favorite things to do was to pick dandelions. We grew up eating dandelion salad—fresh dandelions, olive oil, wine vinegar, salt & pepper, and hard boiled eggs. Everyone loved it, and the season for having the salads was very short—April. By May, the leaves would turn tough and bitter and you could no longer eat them. The earlier they were picked the better they would be. On any given Saturday or Sunday in April, grandma could be found walking all over town, shopping bag in tow, picking dandelions. We could hardly wait for dinner those nights knowing what a treat we were in for.

One weekend my Aunt Di and my cousin Janice came out to visit us as they frequently did. My dad would pick them up on a

Friday after work. They lived in Chicago, and they would spend the weekend with us, and then Sunday afternoon Uncle George would drive out to pick them up. Aunt Di was crazy about dandelions. She could eat more of them, and faster, too, then anyone I ever knew. That Saturday, Mr. Walker had stopped by to chat with dad. Since his wife and daughter were in Colorado visiting relatives, and it was nearly supper time, dad asked Mr. Walker to stay and have supper with us. Mom set an extra plate and we all sat down to eat. Knowing Aunt Di would be here for supper, grandma had spent the entire morning picking more dandelions than usual. We had an especially big bowl of them that day. After everyone had gotten a helping, the large bowl came around to Aunt Di and she proceeded to pile the rest on her plate. It was almost spilling off the sides. She began to eat, never once pausing to take a breath. She just kept eating away, never looking up either. Mr. Walker seemed to notice how she was devouring the salad. Now we all noticed it, too, but we didn't think much about it because we were used to it by now knowing how she loved them. Suddenly, when her plate is just about empty, Aunt Di looks up, and with a half mouthful of food, exclaims loudly and seriously, "Boy, these dandelions sure aren't very good today." With that, Mr. Walker, with a bewildered look on his face, leaned over to my dad and said, "Boy, I'd sure hate to see how she'd eat them if she thought they were good." We all had a good laugh over that, including Aunt Di. Many times over the years, we've teased her about that.

Grandma loved to crochet. I can still picture her sitting in her room, or in front of the television, crocheting for hours. She was always making someone slippers, and believe me, we all loved getting them. The floors in our house were cold, and the slippers she made were warm and toasty. She also used to make lots of doilies for mom, and even potholders. She tried many times to teach me how to crochet, but somehow I never had the patience to learn. I preferred to watch her do it. Over the years, I came to regret that I never learned how. It would have been something to pass on to my daughter and granddaughter.

Grandma also loved movies and because she did, Tommy and I got to go to a lot of movies with her when she lived with us. And because the movie theaters always showed a double feature, we saw lots of movies. Saturday afternoons, mom would give us about $5.00 and we would take the bus into Harvey to the theater. The bus stop was about six blocks away and to get there we had to take a path that cut through a farmer's yard. This farmer raised geese that roamed free.. Every time we walked down this path, the geese would attack, chasing and pecking. We'd run like mad to escape them, grandma all the while saying her familiar, "Oy yoy yoy" every step of the way. After escaping the geese, we'd finally catch the bus, but always in the back of my mind was the return trip where we'd once again encounter the dreaded geese. At the theater, we'd pay the admission, buy popcorn and candy, and heed mom's final words before we walked out the door: "Don't forget to save money for the bus ride home." We always did, except one time. We must not have been counting the money very good as we spent it, because as we got to the bus station we realized we didn't have any money left for the three bus fares. That was one of the few times I can remember grandma getting mad at us. "Oy, yoy, yoy, how could you spend all the money. Your mama is going to be mad at me, too." Grandma said if it was day time she would have made all of us walk the seven miles home (she loved walking), but because it was about 8:00 at night, and very dark, that was out of the question. Some nice elderly woman overheard our plight and gave us a dime to call home. We thanked her profusely and then called mom to tell her what happened. She had to drive all the way out to pick us up, and while she wasn't overly pleased about it, she just gave us a stern warning to be more careful about the money the next time. As the saying goes, all's well that end's well, and for me it really ended well, because I didn't have to deal with the geese chasing me again on the return walk home from the bus stop.

We loved the rare nights when both mom and dad would go out. Grandma loved television and we'd sit for hours with her and watch TV, tell stories and eat snacks. And best of all, she wouldn't let Tommy be mean to me. She'd really let him have it if he tried anything. I can still hear her broken English asking, "Why you be so mean to your sister. That not nice." She had a way of making him feel bad, and for the rest of the night he'd be extra nice to me.

There was only one thing I ever knew grandma to be afraid

of and that was snakes. How she would panic when she would see one. I can still hear her way out in the garden when she'd come across one. "Oy, yoy, yoy" she'd scream wildly until mom or dad would come out and kill the snake for her, if she hadn't already scared it off with her screaming. One day while at the Woolworth's dime store, we saw a plastic snake. Tommy said, "Hey, Linda, look at this. Couldn't we have fun playing tricks on grandma?" "Yeah, lets buy it." So we did, and later that day, when she was sitting out on the front porch swing, taking a break from working in the garden, Tommy and I came out to talk to her, and while I had her distracted, Tommy slipped the plastic snake out of his pocket and placed it right by her feet. We then went into the house and waited. A few minutes passed and then we heard the most blood curdling scream. Grandma was hysterical. Both mom and dad came out to see what was wrong. The minute dad walked out on the porch he spotted the snake and knew immediately it wasn't real. After he convinced grandma that it was only plastic, she finally calmed down. Mom and dad were absolutely furious with us, and we honestly did feel bad about it, too. We apologized over and over to grandma and promised we would never do it again. I think it was probably the single meanest thing I ever did to anyone. To this day I still feel bad that we played such a mean trick on her.

When grandma came to live with us she had a dog that she brought with her, a white shaggy looking dog named Beauty. She was beautiful, but not the nicest dog. Many times I'd try to play with her but she would always snap at me. Mom said she just wasn't used to being around kids. But grandma loved that dog, so we kept her. She was getting quite old and one day we came home from school and mom said Beauty had died. I felt bad, especially for grandma, but can't say I really missed the dog. We also had a cat named Smarty. Now Smarty was a cool cat but she was a female and it seemed like every few months she had another litter of kittens. I guess back then people didn't pay good money to have their pet spayed or neutered. Dad was really getting annoyed with the constant new litter of kittens. I came home from school one day and when I asked mom where Smarty was she said, "Smarty ran away" and then quickly changed the subject by asking me how my school day had been. It never occurred to me to question why she would think Smarty had run away. After all, she was there that morning before I left for school and it was not unusual for her to disappear for long periods of time. It wasn't till many years later that I found out she had taken her to the local pound.

Now while I'm on the subject of pets, I must mention Ringy. When we purchased the big house, along with the two old barns, we also acquired Ringy. Ringy was, at that time, about 3 years old according to the previous owners. He was black, white, and brown spotted, very scrawny, and he had the saddest eyes I'd ever seen. The prior owners kept him in a dog house that was out behind one of the barns facing the field. They left him for us saying they couldn't take him and didn't know what to do with him. They also said that Ringy had never been loose, not even once. "Just leave him tied up. He's used to it," they said. "Feed and water him once a day and he'll be no trouble for you." And so we did. For a couple of years mom would go out just before supper every night and bring Ringy a pot of food and fresh water. He would jump all over you and it was hard to get the food to him. His poor tail would wag so hard I wouldn't have been surprised if it just fell off. In the winter, dad would put some fresh straw in his dog house to keep him warm. For some reason, I just don't think it occurred to any of us to let him loose. The sad thing, too, was that he not only was tied up, but for the most part, he hardly ever saw anyone because he was behind the barn. In the winter, the only person he'd ever see was mom when she would go out there to bring him his food, unless it was a day when Tommy and I headed to the ice pond. Ringy would come out, bark and jump for a minute and then head right back inside his dog house where it was nice and warm. In the summer, it was a different story. On the days when Tommy and I would go out to play in the ditch out back, digging out our villages in the sand, Ringy would see us and go crazy. Sometimes I thought he would strangle himself because of the way he jumped around. It was quite pitiful.

One summer day, Tommy and I were coming back from the ditch and when Ringy saw us he started going wild. We decided to go and pet him but he was so hyper we could barely get near him. Thereafter, each time on our way back from the ditch, we'd stop and try to play with him a little. He wasn't mean, he just got so excited at seeing people. At supper one night, just after mom had brought him his food and water, Tommy asked mom, "Tomorrow can we let Ringy loose, just for a while?" "Please say yes," I begged. We were really starting to feel sorry for him. I'm not sure what took us so long to realize a dog shouldn't be tied up like that. At first she said she didn't think so. "He's not used to it," she said. "He's probably better off just leaving him alone." But we were persistent and after several days of pestering her, she finally said okay if dad agreed, and he did. We could hardly wait till morning. We raced outside and while Tommy held him down, which wasn't easy, I unhooked the chain. Within a split second, Ringy was free. I can still picture him running around like he was crazy. He ran around and around, back and forth. I just don't think he knew what to make of it. After running around the yard for an hour or so, he suddenly took off into the field. He kept running until we couldn't see him any more. Night time came and Ringy hadn't come back, not even for his supper that mom put out for him. The next morning still no Ringy. We were really getting worried.

Several more days passed and there still was no sign of him. Mom continued to put out fresh food and water, just in case he showed up. About four or five days after we let him loose, we were sitting in the breakfast nook on a Sunday morning having our breakfast, when we heard a faint noise, like a moan. It happened several more times. We all heard it and finally went out to the back porch to see where the noise was coming from. And there by the back porch steps lay Ringy. He could barely move, let alone walk. He was obviously very sick. Dad picked him up and brought him in the house. He laid him down in the kitchen in a small bed mom quickly fixed for him. All night he moaned softly. He was definitely in a lot of pain. It was Sunday, but dad said first thing Monday morning we would get him to a vet. Dad thought that possibly he had been hit by a car. It was just the saddest thing. In the morning Ringy seemed even worse. Dad called his office and said he would be a little late. He placed Ringy in the car and took him to the vet. That was the last time we would ever see him. The vet said Ringy had distemper and there was no chance at all to make him better. He said the humane thing to do was to put him to sleep. I cried myself to sleep that night. I felt so guilty, like it was our fault he was dead. If we hadn't let Ringy loose, he'd still be alive. But dad tried to make me see it in a different light. "Linda, you mustn't feel guilty. Ringy was not happy being tied up. Dogs should have a better life than that. You and Tommy tried to give him that better life. And just remember, his final days were probably the happiest he had ever known—to be free." I felt better after that talk, but my heart still ached for a mangy little dog who just wanted a little attention—and to be free. I asked mom if dogs go to heaven. She said she didn't know for sure. Well, I think they do go to heaven and Ringy is there having a wonderful time, free and happy forever.

One Saturday, Dad's younger brother, Charley, calls to say he will be driving out to pay us a visit that afternoon. Uncle Charley lives in Chicago, and Tommy and Linda always love when he comes to visit. He is in his early thirties and still single, and he is fun and likes to do things and tell stories and make us laugh. When Dad made his barrel of wine in the fall, Uncle Charley would come out and help press the grapes. Uncle Charley could fix anything—he was a TV repairman by trade, and at some point during his visit he could be seen sitting at the kitchen table fixing a radio or an appliance. He often arrived in a new car, and then off they'd all go for a drive into the country. And then he almost always spent at least an hour playing catch with Tommy. Mom always prepared a special meal that she knew Uncle Charley would like. It was well known in the family that Uncle Charley had a delicate stomach—he suffered from ulcers for as long as the kids could remember. They used to think he chewed gum a lot, and were surprised later when they realized those were antacid pills he was always chewing.

When Uncle Charley arrives that hot July afternoon, he does not have a new car this time, but he has something far better: he has a brand new, reel-to-reel tape recorder! None of us, not even mom and dad, have ever seen one of these machines before, and we certainly do not know anyone who owns one. Well, for Tommy and Linda, this is the greatest invention in the history of the world. First, Uncle Charley lets everybody talk into the microphone to say just a few words—"Hi, I'm Linda, I'm 9 years old"—"Hi, I'm Tommy, Linda's older and much smarter brother"—then he patiently shows the kids how to control the various knobs for recording, playing, and rewinding. And when the adults have had enough, Uncle Charley tells Tommy and Linda that they can play with it themselves.

They spend every minute of that Saturday recording their voices over and over. Tommy is a big Chicago White Sox fan and he loves to listen to Bob Elson announce the games on the radio. Almost immediately, he begins pretending he is Bob Elson, assuming an exaggerated radio tone of voice and barking out the play-by-play.

"It's the bottom of the 9th, Sox down three to nothing, bases loaded. Minoso swings. It's a long drive...back back BACK. It's a HOME RUN, SOX WIN! SOX WIN! SOX WIN!" When he listens to the playback later, Tommy is a little disappointed that his voice doesn't quite have the smooth Bob Elson sound.

Hours later, when it is time for Uncle Charley to head home, the kids thank him for all the fun with his new machine, and Uncle Charley promises Tommy that he won't erase his play-by-play routine.

Everybody says their good byes, then Uncle Charley gets into his car and starts to back out of the driveway, and everyone is standing in the lawn, waving. He pauses for a moment, pops a pill into his mouth, while our whole family continues to stand there waving. Uncle Charley pulls forward again, stops the car and gets out. He reaches into the back seat, picks up the tape recorder, and hands it to Tommy.

"You kids can keep it until I come back, in a month or so," he says.

Tommy and Linda are in disbelief. "Oh, no, Uncle Charley," Linda says. "What if we accidentally break it?"

Uncle Charley just shrugs. "If you break it, I'll fix it. Just have fun with it."

And with that there is another round of goodbyes and thank you's and more waving...and then he heads off down Hamlin Avenue on his way back to Chicago.

For the next month, Tommy and Linda spend most of their waking life playing with Uncle Charley's tape recorder. Linda, who loves to sing and play the piano, records many of her favorite songs, and then spends hours listening. That's when she first realizes she doesn't have a great singing voice. Tommy and Linda also have a lot of fun at Dad's expense. Dad always claimed he never snored, so one day the kids record more than a half hour of continual snoring. He listens to it with amusement, but decides he's heard enough after a few minutes.

Tommy, in addition to calling baseball games, took up calling horse races. Dad had taken the kids to Washington Park many times, and Tommy was particularly taken by the way the track announcer called the race. The Washington Park track announcer always began every race in the exact same way, stretching the word "And" almost a half a block:

"Aaaaaannnnnnnnndddddd....they're OFF!" Tommy practiced that opening for hours, until he thought he had it just right. Then, with the Chicago Sun Times racing line-up in his hands, he would call the race:

"Sir Winston jumps to the lead from the inside, with Sickles Image in close quarters on the rail, followed by Wins-or-Not with jockey Eddie Arcaro in the red silks going to the whip. Around the first turn they go..."

One day, when Linda insisted on having more time with the tape recorder to herself, Tommy comes up with a game that he thinks will please both of them.

"Come on, Linda. We'll play horse racing. You pick a horse, I'll pick a horse, and then we'll bet on who wins. The winner gets to keep the recorder for the rest of the day." Linda looks at him warily at first, but then she agrees. Tommy hands her a list of the horses running in today's first race at Washington Park.

"Who do you like?" Tommy asked.

Linda looks at the racing card for only a moment, and then says, excitedly: "Look, Tommy, there's a horse in this race named 'Charley Boy,' and we're using Uncle Charley's tape recorder. That's who I'm picking."

Tommy agrees it's a good choice. *I wish I had seen that,"* Tommy says. "But I'll let you have Charley Boy, and I'll take this horse called Peanut Gallery. And with that, Tommy starts his call of the race:

"Aaaaaannnnnnnnnd....they're OFF! Charley Boy bolts to the front along the rail and quickly opens up a lead of two lengths. Pot Luck is second by a half length over California Girl, followed closely by Fancy Pants, Big Red, Sherlock, Sunset Sadie, and, bringing up the rear, Peanut Gallery. Around the first turn, Charley Boy stretches his lead to four lengths...."

And so the race goes, with Charley Boy gradually pulling away from the pack. Linda is beside herself with excitement, jumping up and down and cheering her horse. But then, an amazing thing happens. Out of nowhere, here comes Peanut Gallery roaring down the stretch on the outside to overtake the "badly tiring" Charley Boy. Peanut Gallery wins by a nose in a photo finish.

Linda stares at Tommy in disbelief. "You did that on purpose."

"Sorry, Linda. That's horse racing. Anyway, I get to keep the recorder for the rest of the day. Let's bet on the second race."

"No way," she says, and storms out of the room.

The next day Tommy tries again. "Come on, Linda, let's do another race."

"No!"

"Just one. You can have the favorite."

"No!"

"Tell you what...there are twelve horses in this race. You can have eleven of them. Whichever one is left, I'll take that horse."

"I can have eleven horses?"

"Yep."

"And you get just one?"

"Yep." He hands her the racing page, and she checks off eleven horses, leaving for Tommy a horse called Staggering In. And of course, Staggering In breaks dead last and trails the entire field all the way around the track, until a few lengths from the finish line he closes with a rush and wins in another photo finish. Linda glares at Tommy with hatred. She is so angry she can't speak.

"That's horse racing, Linda."

Post Script: Years later, in 1973, Tommy (now Tom) is sitting at a bar in Evanston, Illinois on a Saturday afternoon, with his two children, Lisa and Chris. There is a big TV screen above the bar. Today was the Belmont Stakes, and Tom wouldn't have missed it for the world. This was the third leg of the Triple Crown."

"Tell you what, kids," Tom says. "Let's make a bet for the fun of it. There are 15 horses in the race, and I'll let you kids have every horse but one."

Lisa and Chris think that's a great idea. "Okay, Dad," they say. "That's a bet. Which one do you want?"

"I'll just take the one named Secretariat."

DECK THE HALLS

Christmases at our house were wonderful, and no matter how old I get, I will never forget them. We opened our presents on Christmas Eve and it wasn't until I was much older that I realized most people opened theirs on Christmas Day. Every Christmas Eve mom's sisters and their families would come over. Dad would pick up Aunt Di and Janice, my cousin, on his way home from work. Tommy and I would stare out the dining room window waiting for them to pull in the driveway. It seemed like they would never get here. Janice, who was almost five years younger than me, would be dressed in the most beautiful holiday dress and fancy patent leather shoes. Because she was five years younger than us, Tommy, Kerry, and I weren't (at times) very nice to her. We liked her all right, and she was really cute, but five years is a big difference when you're kids. We would always try to get rid of her and wouldn't let her play with us. She'd go downstairs crying to her mother and next thing, here comes Aunt Di marching up the stairs. She'd grab Kerry and me by the neck and really scold us for being so mean to her daughter, and I guess you really couldn't blame her. We'd promise that we'd be nice to her, but when her mom would leave the room, we'd start all over again. And, of course, Janice would again go tell her mom, and upstairs Auntie would come again, and on and on and on it went.

After dad arrived with Aunt Di and Janice, I'd wait impatiently for Aunt Dee and Uncle Larry to arrive with Kerry, and Grandma Kate (Uncle Larry's mother). Aunt Honey and her family would also come, and, of course, Grandma Mary. Mom always cooked a feast for supper, and baked scrumptious pies, usually pumpkin and raisin, and after we were all stuffed, we'd gather round the piano. Dad would play Christmas Carols and everyone would sit around the tree and sing. Kerry would recite a poem, "Jest for Christmas I'm as Good as I can Be." It was all so festive. Earlier one year, Janice had started taking tap dancing lessons. And that Christmas Eve, after everyone else had arrived, Aunt Di asked Janice to dance for us. And dance she did. Back and forth all over the dining room, just banging those taps on her shoes like mad. She was pretty good and we enjoyed it. ...for a while. Every time she would stop, Aunt Di would say, "Come on, Janice, dance some more." So away she'd go, dancing up another storm. Of course, the floor took a major beating, but, hey, mom had her buffer, remember? She didn't care!

The sun parlor was a large room and dad would always get the biggest Christmas tree he could find, taking up most of the room. Tommy and I would help with the trimming, but mom did most of the work. It was so beautiful I would sometimes just sit and stare at it for hours. They would make all of us wait until midnight to open our presents. It was the longest night of the year. We could only play so much, and then our thoughts would turn back to the presents under the tree. We'd have Tommy go down and ask if we could please open then early. We figured if anyone could talk them into it, it would be him, what with him being everybody's favorite. But he never had any luck either. So wait we did. When midnight finally arrived, we were beside ourselves with joy. Tommy would always hand out the presents. When Kerry and I complained once that we wanted to hand them out, we had to hear, "Tommy's the only boy, let him do it." Fine…as long as we got our gifts. One by one, we'd open our gifts, and the next person could not open a gift until everyone had seen the previous gift that had been opened. This way it took a long time, and that was okay with us. Everyone got to see everything. Late into the night, actually early morning, everyone would leave, except Aunt Di and Janice. They would spend the night and on Christmas Day, Uncle George would come out to pick them up. And mom would always make spaghetti for supper that day, along with fried chicken. Some might say that didn't seem like much of a Christmas Day dinner, but we already had our feast the night before, and besides, it was Uncle George's favorite meal.

One Christmas Tommy got a pair of boxing gloves, actually two pairs, since boxing is no fun without an opponent. And guess who he persuaded to be his opponent? I didn't want to, but he promised we would just spar lightly. When the Christmas tree was taken down, we turned the sun parlor into a boxing ring, put on the gloves, and began boxing. For the first few rounds we had fun. True to his word, he barely touched me. Sometimes he'd pretend like I was actually hurting him, even though I knew I wasn't. One time when I threw a punch, he staggered and fell to the floor. He told me to count to ten and if he didn't get up, then I was the winner. He struggled to his feet by the count of nine, looking dazed and confused, and then he let loose with a blow to my head. Now these gloves were huge cushioned things, almost like wearing a pillow on your hands, but let me tell you, that punch sent me reeling. I went running for mom and told her what Tommy had done to me. "Ma, Tommy slugged me in the face when he promised not to and it really hurt." And ma would yell at him and make him promise never to do it again, and he'd swear it was an accident. "Ma, I'm sorry, I really didn't mean to hit her that hard." Then she'd say, "Linda, Tommy said he was sorry, so stop crying and play. He won't do it any more." Was she kidding or what?

The following day I wanted him to play cutouts with me. "Only if you'll box afterwards," he said. I agreed to give the boxing one more try but told him if he ever hit me hard again I'd never box with him again. Later that day, after playing cutouts, we put on the boxing gloves, laced them up, and started sparring lightly. He threw a really hard punch that luckily missed me.

"You're swinging too hard, Tommy."

"I missed you on purpose," he said. "If I wanted to hit you, believe me, I could."

"You better not."

"Quit talking and fight."

So we continued boxing, and just when I thought he really meant it when he said he wouldn't punch me hard again, he delivered a strong punch to my head that knocked me down. When I got up I went running toward the kitchen where mom was listening to Suppertime Frolic on the radio and frying liver and onions for supper. Yuck, nothing was going right that day.

"Ma, I swear I didn't do it on purpose. I just start boxing and don't realize my own strength. I'm sorry," Tommy explained.

"He didn't mean it, Linda," mom said. "Don't box with him if you don't want to get hurt."

After mom left the room, I told him I quit. He said he'd beat me up if I didn't box with him. "Let's see if I have this straight," I said. "If I box with you, you'll punch me and I'll get hurt, and if I refuse to box, you'll beat me up and I'll get hurt?" Tommy just smiled. What kind of choices were those? I wished at that moment I was bigger and stronger so I could wipe that silly grin off his face.

Mom would always make Tommy and me take a nap, no matter how much we protested, on Christmas Eve because she knew we'd be up very late. Usually about 4:00 she'd send us upstairs and she'd say if we weren't up by 6:00 she'd wake us.

Deck the Halls

One time, Tommy and I were in our rooms and we just couldn't fall asleep. "Hey, Linda, are you sleeping?" "No, I said." He came in my room and we talked for a while. We were probably about six and eight years old at that time. Then he said, "Hey, I have an idea. Lets sneak downstairs and see what mom and dad are doing?" "Yeah, let's go." Quietly, as quiet as one could be with our creaky floors, we tiptoed down the stairs. Just as we got as far as we could go without being seen, we saw dad coming in carrying two sleds — two beautiful sleds. Mom was holding two huge red bows that she placed on the sleds. Then dad put them as far behind the tree as he could and covered them with a sheet. "There, that should do it. I think they're pretty well hidden." Mom smiled, "I can't wait to see their faces. That's all they've been asking Santa for." A punch in the stomach from Tommy couldn't have hurt more. "See Linda," Tommy whispered. "I told you I didn't think there was a Santa but you didn't believe me. Now we both know for sure." We both stared at each other for a second, and without saying a word, we quietly turned and went back upstairs before they saw us. As I lay in bed, the tears came, and as I fell asleep I thought — sometimes just when you think you're pretty clever, it turns out that you're not so clever after all. That was my worst Christmas ever. However, we sure did love the sleds!

Tommy and Linda (ages 4 and 2)

Mom, Dad, Tommy and Linda
1946

Mom and Dad
1951

Linda and Dad at annual Coselinski Day picnic (1950)

Uncle Charley, Dad, Uncle Bill, Uncle Frank, Aunt Ada in Tower Hill, PA 1926

Dad and Uncle Charley
8th Grade Graduation - 1928

Dad, Uncle Charley, Uncle Frank, Uncle Bill in 1943

Dad playing the piano after dinner (1957)

Dad and his beloved 1949 Nash

1954 black/red Nash

With mom and dad, Tommy and Linda on their First Communion Day May, 1950

Tommy and Linda trimming Christmas tree (1955)

Grandpa Leonardo Molin

Grandma Mary (1983)

Grandma Carmella Castellano in 1940. She died several months before I was born.

Mom at age 14 with her sister Inez (Aunt Honey) (1934)

*Kate and Grandma Mary
Christmas Eve at our house (1951)*

Linda with cousin Kerry (1947)

Aunt Di and Janice (1955)

Linda, Janice and Kerry (1955)

The cottage at Honey Lake (1952)   *Aunt Di, Mom, Aunt Honey, Aunt Dee, Grandma Mary (Mid 1950's)*

Aunt Honey and Uncle George, Aunt Dee and Uncle Larry, Mom and Dad, Aunt Di and Uncle George (1962) Picture taken at Kerry's Wedding

Doris Willmer (1955)

Homecoming Dance 1957
Back row: Judy Porter & Linda
Front: Sue Donnelly & Barbara Lugar

*Linda and Sue
(1957)*

*Singing group "Teen Toppers" performing on stage at our 8th grade
graduation dance (1956)
Barbara Lugar, Judy Pagan, Donna Olson, Sharon Kennedy, Linda, Judy
Porter, and Sue Donnelly*

A Honey of a Lake

The summer before my eighth birthday, our summer vacation changed. And what a great change it was. Kerry's grandma Kate owned a cottage just outside Burlington, Wisconsin on Honey Lake. It was about a three hour drive from our house in Markham to the town of Burlington. For a number of years, our grandma Mary used to go up to the cottage and spend several weeks each summer with Kate. Kerry also used to spend a few weeks up there with the two grandma's when her parents would go up there. Aunt Dee decided Kerry was old enough to spend a couple months up there with the grandmas. She asked mom if Tommy and I would like to spend a month or so up there, too. I'd never been away from home, not ever, so even though I was dying to go, I was also a little apprehensive at first. It was agreed that we could go, but if after a week or so we were homesick, mom and dad would drive up there and pick us up. With that reassurance, we were all ready to go. A few days after school let out in June, mom packed clothes for Tommy and me and drove us up to Aunt

Dee's. We spent the night there and in the morning Uncle Larry drove all of us up to Wisconsin. And for the next five years, the cottage would become our summer playground, always returning by August 1, the start of dad's two week vacation. No matter how much we loved the cottage, and believe me, we did, we still wouldn't miss dad's vacation for anything.

The ride seemed endless. We spent most of the drive talking nonstop about all the things we were going to do over the next month. Once we crossed the state line into Wisconsin, the ride became more interesting. Never having been in Wisconsin before, I was amazed at how beautiful the state was. I stared out the window taking in all the scenery. Mile after mile of gentle rolling hills graced the landscape. And dairy cows, lots of them, filled every farmers' pasture. Guess that's why they call it the Dairy State. The closer we got to the cottage the more excited we became, and by the time we were nearing the town of Burlington, I could hardly contain myself. The drive to Honey Lake took about another 10 minutes, and as we drove along the two lane paved highway, I just knew I was going to love being at the cottage and would not get homesick and want to go home

Uncle Larry made a left turn onto a gravel road. Straight ahead was a huge hill, and that hill would become one of my fondest childhood memories at Honey Lake. The cottage sat at the top of that hill, and to go anywhere, there was always the hill to be climbed when we returned. Sometimes we'd climb up and down a dozen times a day without any thought that it was quite steep. At the top of the hill, Uncle Larry made another left turn onto a small, narrow road that barely passed for a road. It was a mixture of gravel and dirt, and a hundred feet later, I got my first glimpse of the cottage. It was a white frame house, with red trim and a dark reddish roof. The front had an enclosed porch, which we would come to love. When we pulled into the driveway, the two grandmas came running out to greet us. It was so good to see them both, especially my own grandma. She had gone to the cottage a few weeks before, and I really missed her.

Once inside, Tommy and I were given the grand tour. It wasn't very big, but I don't think I even noticed. From the front porch you entered the living room. They had a small television, but Honey Lake was so far in the country, that the few channels they did get had very poor reception. We didn't care. There were so many more fun things to do. There were two bedrooms. One bedroom was for Aunt Dee and Uncle Larry when they came out on weekends. When they weren't at the cottage, then grandma Kate would sleep in there. The other bedroom had one double bed and one twin bed, and that's where Kerry, Tommy and I slept. It had a small bathroom, with no tub or shower. The kitchen was the largest of the rooms. It had a small cooking area, and the rest of the room was filled with a large table at one end, and at the opposite end of the room was an open area. A daybed was against one wall and that is where grandma Mary would sleep.

Outside, the yard had a shed out in back, and the only thing memorable about that shed was the hornets nest. The place was loaded with hornets. Year after year Uncle Larry would try to get rid of them, and the following year they'd all be back, building more nests. It really was creepy, and I rarely, if ever, went near it. The yard had lots of trees, and out back a hammock was tied between two of them. There were perhaps seven or eight other cottages in the area, but most of them were empty during the week. On weekends the placed filled up.

To get to the lake, we would run down the big hill, go about one block, and there it was. I remember the first time I saw it. It was bigger than I expected it to be and I couldn't believe that I'd get to swim there every single day for as long as we stayed at the cottage. It wasn't the cleanest lake near the shore. We had to wade through seaweed, but we didn't care. Once we got past the seaweed, it was great. Well, sort of great, that is. There were snapping turtles you had to get passed, too. More than once we all had a toe nipped, but again, it was worth it just to spend the days swimming. There was a big raft about 30 yards out that we would swim to. Sometimes we'd have races to and from the raft. We'd also dive off of it, although for me, I think it was more like "jumping" off it. One of the most amazing things about Honey Lake was the fact that we were just about the only ones at the lake during the week. We virtually had the whole place to ourselves. It was paradise. We could run, jump, holler, act silly, do anything we wanted. No one would see us. We began to think of it as "our" lake.

Before we left home, mom would give Tommy and me each

$20 for spending money. When she handed us the money, she'd always say, "Now don't spend it all at once. Remember, it has to last all summer. You cannot ask either grandma for any money." We would assure her we'd be careful, and I think we were. About a block past the lake were three stores. One was a tavern that we never went into, an ice cream shop we occasionally went into, and a small grocery store where we spent quite a bit of time (and money). There we would buy candy, soda pop, ice cream and popsicles. Lots of popsicles. Every day when we'd leave the lake, we'd stop at the store to get a treat. It was owned by a lady named Eunice Badalamente, and over the years we got to know her quite well. Before we'd leave to go home each year, we'd always stop one last time to say goodbye to her. And one of the first things we'd do upon arriving the following summer would be to run down to her store and say hi. We really liked her, and I think she liked us as well.

There was a creek that ran under the main road in town. When we would go to the store we'd have to walk over a bridge, and we even managed to make the bridge fun. On the way back from the store, after finishing our popsicles, we'd lean over the bridge, one of us at each end, and one in the middle, and on the count of three, we'd drop our sticks into the creek and watch the current carry them under the bridge. We'd then run across the street to the other side, lean over the bridge, and wait to see which of our sticks would appear first and win the race. Such simple things made us happy.

We usually got to the lake about 10:00 in the morning and we'd stay until about 3:00. If we got hungry, we'd take a break and go get something to eat at the store. Sometimes grandma Kate would send food with us and other times we'd just swim all day and go for our snack afterwards. Tommy used to go once a day, usually around noon, to get a newspaper, the Chicago Sun-Times, so he could read the sports section. I remember how surprised, and glad, he was when he found out he could get the Chicago paper at Honey Lake. The day would go by quickly and by the time supper rolled around, we were starved. Grandma Kate did all the cooking, and she always made plenty.

At the bottom of the hill was a house where an elderly lady named Hilda lived. Hilda raised lilies and they were not only beautiful flowers, they were her pride and joy. She would enter them in flower shows, and most of the time she would win first prize. Absolutely nobody was allowed in or even near her garden. We were always in awe of these flowers, and on one particular trip, Tommy decided he would pick a few. "Hey, Linda, Kerry, wait here. I'm going to go and get each of you a couple of Hilda's flowers." "No," we both said. "If you get caught, you're going to get in big trouble," I told him. We both warned him, but once he gets something in his head, there's no changing his mind. Kerry and I kept on walking. There was no way we were going to just stand there in front of Hilda's house while he was in her garden. Tommy started picking her flowers. Suddenly, we heard a yell. The next thing Tommy came running past us, non-stop, full-speed ahead. He didn't slow down until he reached the top of the hill and was out of sight from Hilda's house. After Kerry and I got back to the cottage, Tommy told us that while he was picking the flowers, Hilda opened her door and started to come out. "I don't know whether or not she saw me but she yelled, 'Hey, you, get out of there. Leave my flowers alone.' I ran as fast as I could away from there," he said. He made us promise we wouldn't tell grandma. The following evening, the two grandmas decided to go for a walk. They were gone about an hour, and when they came back, grandma Kate said, "We saw Hilda out in her yard, and stopped to visit with her. She was really mad because she said some kid the day before picked some of her flowers." The three of us just sort of looked at each other but sat quietly as Kate continued. "Hilda said she didn't get a real good look at the boy but noticed he was wearing a red shirt, and if she ever finds him, she'll report him to the police for stealing and trespassing." After hearing this, Tommy quietly disappeared into the bedroom, picked up his red shirt that was flung over the back of a chair, and put it in the bottom of his suitcase, never to be worn again that summer.

 Every night we'd sit at the kitchen table and play some kind of a game, usually Bunco. And almost every night Kate would make us Black Cows, or as they are more commonly known, root beer floats. It was the perfect ending to a perfect day. By 10:00 we'd all be tired and ready for bed.

 On weekends, Aunt Dee and Uncle Larry would come out.

They would arrive on Friday night and go back to the city late Sunday afternoon. This would be the only time we would go into Burlington. Neither of the grandmas drove, so other than getting a few of the essentials at the local store, i.e. bread and milk, they'd make a list of what they needed and then on the weekends we'd all drive into Burlington. While they went to the supermarket, Tommy, Kerry and I could walk around the town. They had a dimestore and we used to browse around there for a while. Then we would meet them at a place called the Carousel. It was an ice cream parlor, and more than the ice cream, I remember the color of the place—-pink and white. They had an awning out front that was pink and white, and the tables and chairs were also pink and white. And the clerks working there wore pink and white. It was so pretty. We'd meet Aunt Dee and Uncle Larry there and they'd buy us all ice cream, any kind we wanted. It was delicious and best of all, we didn't have to spend any of our own money on it.

The summer between 7th and 8th grade, Kerry and I were 12 years old, and quite naïve to say the least. Back then there was no such thing as sex education in school, and few parents talked about it, certainly not mine or Kerry's mom. What we learned we learned from other girls, but mostly we weren't interested in that sort of stuff. One morning we awoke to a very dismal day. Instead of the usual bright sunshine, dark clouds loomed overhead. It was just beginning to rain, and at breakfast grandma said we could not go to the beach until the sky cleared. By mid morning we were in the midst of a heavy thunderstorm. Rainy days were rare, but when they occurred, we found other ways to spend the day.

The front porch was perfect for such days. Kate had an old victrolla that had to be cranked up, and we'd spend the day playing over and over the few 78 rpm records she had. We used to love taking turns cranking it up, and it was there that we learned one of our favorite songs. I used to sing it to my own kids, and to this day, I still sing it for my grandkids, and everyone still gets a kick out of it. It's called "I'm My Own Grandpa." We also learned a song called "My Grandfather's Clock," and that too, I still love to sing for my grandkids. One of our favorite things to do was play Amateur Hour, where we'd all take turns singing, dancing, or whatever else came to mind. Sometimes we'd even act out scenes from movies. Never at a loss for something to do, the day went by quickly.

It was late in the afternoon when the rain stopped and the sky once again was bright and sunny. Kerry and I decided, even though it was too late to go to the beach, we'd take a walk down to the store, visit with Eunice, and get some ice cream. It was still a couple of hours before supper. Tommy, having tired several hours earlier of listening to us sing, was busy listening to a White Sox baseball game on the radio and didn't want to go. He asked us to bring him back a piece of candy, and we said we would. We ran out of the house, still singing, raced down the hill and sauntered happily into the store. We talked to Eunice for a bit, bought two popsicles and a Hershey bar for Tommy. Then we started back home. We were just about to the bridge when a car pulled up and called to us, "Hey, girls, can you tell me how to get to Honey Creek?" We started to give him some directions when he interrupted, "You're too far away. Come closer so I can hear you." So we did. We walked across the street to his car. Then Kerry, because she knew the area better than me, started to give him the directions to Honey Creek. While she was talking, I happened to notice a funny movement of his arm, so being curious, I leaned in the window a little, and when I looked down, I had the biggest shock in all my 12 years on this earth. I quickly nudged Kerry and she looked at me, then followed my gaze downward. And then she gasped. There he was, totally exposed, and to steal a line from a Seinfeld episode, 'he was treating his body like it was an amusement park.' He heard us both gasp and then quickly said a few things I won't repeat here. With that, Kerry and I took off running. We were up that hill and at the cottage in record time. Needless to say, we didn't race our popsicle sticks that day.

Once we got to the cottage we went running through the door, totally out of breath and babbling so fast no one could understand what we were saying. After they calmed us down, we told them what had just happened. Now Kerry and I knew what he was doing was wrong, but like I said, we were quite naïve, so we thought it was funny more than anything. We were laughing as we described the incident to the two grandmas. I assure you, though, they weren't amused. I'll never forget the look of horror on both the grandmas faces. Grandma Mary just kept saying "Oy yoy yoy." After we convinced them we were all right, Grandma Kate said she'd be back in a little bit. She was going down to see Hilda and use her phone (we didn't have one at the cottage). She said we must stay at the cottage with Grandma Mary and Tommy, and she forbid us to go anywhere. Frankly, we thought the grandmas were overreacting. She came back about 45 minutes later and said she had talked with a policeman, giving him the details of what had occurred. They put out a search but to my knowledge, they never did find him. For a few days, the grandmas wouldn't let Kerry and I leave the cottage, and when they finally did, they made certain Tommy was always with us. And to this day, when Kerry and I talk about the cottage, the "flasher," as we called him, will eventually be mentioned.

 During seventh grade, I became good friends with a girl who was fairly new at our school, Carol Hayward. She was from Long Beach, California and her family had moved here the year before. She was just about the nicest girl I had ever met. On our last day of school before summer vacation, we only had half a day of school. Getting out at noon, Carol came home with me to spend the afternoon. I still remember the fun we had. We practiced doing "cheers" in the front yard, and twirling batons, and talked non stop about being eighth graders in the fall. She had supper with us and later that night we drove her home. "I'll call you as soon as I get back from Honey Lake," I said. "Okay, don't forget.

Maybe we can get together again before school starts. Have fun at the cottage." "Thanks," I said. "I hope you have a nice summer, too." We gave each other a quick hug, said goodbye, and I got back in the car. As mom drove off, I waved one last goodbye before Carol turned and walked into her house. I would never see her again.

We arrived at the cottage in mid June and immediately got into the routine of the past few summers. We still loved the cottage and everything about being up there. It would soon be the 4th of July and we were looking forward to Aunt Dee and Uncle Larry coming up. They were going to take us into Burlington to see the fireworks, and afterwards, stop at the Carousel. They arrived on the 3rd, and as promised, they took us to see fireworks, followed by ice cream. Then back at the house, they played Bunco with us. The following morning they left to go back home. After they were gone we couldn't wait to get to the beach because we hadn't been there for two days. It was a hot day and the water felt wonderful. At noon, Tommy said he was going to the store to get the newspaper. He said he'd bring us back a bottle of pop. Kerry and I were out on the raft when Tommy came back. He started calling out to me but I couldn't quite hear what he was saying. He yelled real loud, "Hey, Linda, don't you know a girl named Carol Hayward? Isn't she your friend?" "Yes, she is," I hollered back. "Why?" "Her picture's on the front page of the paper. You better come here quick and see it," he said. I quickly jumped off the raft and started swimming to shore. I was excited thinking something great had happened for her to be on the front page. When I got to shore, Tommy handed me the paper. There was her picture, so pretty, and there in big headlines it said, **"GIRL KILLED BY SKYROCKET."** I almost became hysterical. The article went on to say that Carol had been in her backyard with her family. A few houses down, some neighbors were playing with fireworks. This particular skyrocket was supposed to go straight up vertically when lit. Instead, it misfired and went horizontally, across several back yards and hit Carol in the stomach, exploding on impact. She died almost immediately. Needless to say, I didn't feel like swimming any more that day. That evening Grandma Mary walked with me down to the store. They had a pay phone in the store and I wanted to call home and talk to mom. She was glad I called because she wasn't sure if I had heard about it. She told me she and dad were going to the wake. I called her again several days later and she said all Carol's classmates were at the wake and there wasn't a dry eye in the place. As the days passed, the summer got back to normal, but it never was quite the same for me. I still had fun, but Carol was never far from my mind.

    The following summer would be the last time we'd go to the cottage. Kerry and I would be starting high school and Tommy his second year. By now we were all busy with our own lives, doing things with our friends, and it seemed like we just outgrew the desire to spend so much time away from home. Our final year was rather bittersweet. Although we had fun, a part of us was still longing to be home. That summer our cousin Janice also joined us. She was now old enough to spend the summer there. Aunt Di and Uncle George drove her out, and Aunt Di's parting words as they left were, "Don't you kids be mean to her. And watch out for her." Of course, we said we would, and we actually did. We were older now and we didn't find her annoying. I guess we realized that she just wanted to join in with her older cousins, and that summer we were more than willing to let her. I guess we were growing up, too. The summer went by quickly, and as usual, we left in time to be home for dad's two week vacation in August. We still hadn't outgrown that. When we left the cottage that summer, it would be 45 years until I would return to Honey Lake.

Love Thy Neighbor

As a young girl, my closest friend was my next door neighbor, Doris Willmer. The youngest of five kids, she was two years older than me. Her family was very poor, and totally dysfunctional, but that made no difference to me. The father, Frank, drank too much, but despite his drinking, we liked him. He was so good to all the neighborhood kids. Her mother, Minnie, was the hardest working person, other than my mom, that I ever knew. That poor woman spent her life cleaning the little house they had, and the rest of the family spent their life messing it up. There was no carpeting anywhere in the house, just bare wooden planks that she spent her life mopping up. The kitchen was the exception. It had linoleum that always looked worn and faded from constant scrubbing. About every two years she'd get new linoleum and she'd be so happy. In no time at all though, you'd never know it was only a few months old. As fast as she'd get something clean, her family would be making a mess. She never complained, although it wouldn't have done her any good even if she did. She, too, was always friendly, despite how tired she always seemed. Her only break from cleaning and cooking, was when she'd come over and sit with mom in the breakfast nook and have a cup of coffee. I think she looked forward to that more than anything. She'd ramble on endlessly about such mundane things as the weather or the latest gossip in the neighborhood. Mom would patiently sit and listen, and keep refilling her cup of coffee. And though I'm sure mom would rather be getting back to her own work, she always made time for Minnie.

At least once a week Frank would send one of the kids over, usually Doris, and ask to borrow money, usually $10.00 "until payday." Now looking back, that was very strange considering Frank didn't work. Where he got his money I don't know, but oddly, he always paid back whatever he borrowed. And borrowing didn't stop at money; a day didn't go by that they didn't ask for something... a cup of sugar or flour, a loaf of bread, stick of butter, a little salt, etc. But again, a few days later, they'd return what they had borrowed. And so it went for all the years we lived next to them. They were the only family I ever knew to have an outhouse. Other than running water (cold only) in the house, they had no plumbing whatsoever. And while I couldn't imagine someone not having a bathroom, for the most part none of us gave it much thought that smack in the middle of their back yard stood the outhouse. Once every year or so, I'd see the two boys, Gayland and Albert, outside digging a big hole. The next day the outhouse would be in the new location where they had been digging the previous day. And where the outhouse had stood would be a big heap of dirt that eventually would flatten and blend in with the rest of the yard. There was no grass in the back yard, just dirt and weeds.

And while I played, Doris worked. She always had to help her mom with chores. The other kids made the mess, she cleaned up. Every time we'd be out playing, her mother would yell out the door for her to come home because there was work to be done. I felt so sorry for her. She, too, despite everything, was always cheerful. I guess it just ran in the family. When you don't have much, maybe you don't expect much. When she wasn't helping out at home, we had a great time together. She was a good friend.

One Saturday morning, Frank Willmer comes over to repay the $10 he had borrowed last week to pay the electric bill. Tommy and Linda are sleeping, mom is straightening the house, grandma is already out working in the garden, so dad, who is on the back porch trying to fix mom's washing machine gets stuck with Frank. He asks dad if he might pour him a shot of whiskey, "to calm my nerves," Frank says.

"What's the problem," dad asks him.

"It's Minnie," Frank says—his wife. "She says she's leaving me."

"Why is that, Frank?" Dad has heard this many times before.

"She says I drink."

Dad laughs. "And when did she discover this?"

"Well, I got drunk on our wedding night, 35 years ago." Frank shrugs, knocks back the shot, then pours another one. "How about one for you, Tom?" he asks. Dad tells him it's too early, even for Early Times.

After sharing with dad the usual list of complaints and injustices, Frank gets up to go. At the door, he puts an arm on dad's shoulder.

"You're a good man, Tom," he says. "The best neighbor anyone could ask for. The day you moved here, I told Minnie: Minnie, I can tell he's a good man. If you don't believe me, ask her, she'll tell you. Why don't you come over with me right now and ask her."

Dad explains that he has some things Betty wants him to do around the house. At the door, Frank pauses. "Do you think you could spare $5.00 till payday?" Dad reaches in his pocket and finds only the ten that Frank has just repaid. "Here, Frank. Pay Betty back as soon as you can."

"You're a good man, Tom," Frank says as he walks out the porch door and down the lawn to his house. "I've always said you were a good man."

About an hour later, Doris comes running over to tell us that her brother, Gayland, is having a seizure and they are worried he will swallow his tongue. Mom, Tommy, and Linda go over to see if they can help.

Hamlin Avenue

There lays Gayland on the floor in the living room, his face blue, eyes rolled back, arms and legs writhing, with Minnie trying to get him to take a drink of water. Nobody else seems to be paying attention. That's because this has happened many times to Gayland and they are used to it by now. While Minnie continues to revive Gayland, Doris grabs a broom and starts sweeping. Now Frank walks out of one of the bedrooms. He has changed clothes, spruced up a bit. In his fingers he clutches the ten dollar bill he had returned and then reborrowed. What he wants to know now, from Betty, is whether she thinks dad will either drive him to the liquor store, or alternatively, call him a cab. Otherwise, he will walk to Midlothian. Mom tells him he'll have to ask dad himself

Linda goes into the kitchen where Betty Lou, older sister of Doris, is having breakfast. On the table is a huge bowl of sugar. With a tablespoon, Betty Lou is spreading about an inch of sugar on a slice of Wonder bread. She asks if Linda would like a piece, but Linda says she just had breakfast. Then Betty Lou asks Linda if she'd like to see her boobies. Before Linda can answer, Betty Lou yanks up her shirt and grins. "Bet you wish you had these," she says. Linda pretends she hasn't heard Betty Lou and says something else. Betty Lou pulls her shirt down just as Tommy walks into the kitchen. He, too, declines her offer of sugar bread. "You know what Helen Gernenz eats for breakfast every morning?" Betty Lou asks. Helen, she says, eats one dozen eggs, a pound of bacon, and a loaf of buttered toast. Helen, who lives on the next block, can no longer ride a bike because she weighs more than 400 pounds. But she still takes walks, and when you run into her on the street she is friendly to everyone. She always has a few candy bars in her pocket and she never fails to offer you one.

Dad comes over to see what is going on. We all walk into the Willmer kitchen and there is Gayland, all recovered, sitting at the table, looking like he just woke up. Albert, or "PeeWee" as we called him, sits on the floor putting shells into his shot gun. Later, he'll be out in the field "hunting for birds." Minnie and Doris continue cleaning the house. All is back to "normal" in the Willmer household...for awhile. Mom, dad, Tommy and Linda go back home.

GIRLS JUST WANT TO HAVE FUN

As much as I liked Doris, going to school gave me a chance to meet and make new friends. A few of them were extra special: Susan Donnelly, Barbara Lugar, Judy Porter, and a little later, Donna Olson. And while the five of us were very close, I considered Sue and Barb my best friends. We were inseparable. Sue's mom and dad were two of the coolest people I'd ever met. Her dad reminded me of Jackie Gleason, not only in appearance, but he was always saying or doing something funny... sort of like dad. Her mother was the classiest looking mother I'd ever seen. She always had on the nicest clothes, she always wore makeup, and her hair looked like she had just come out of a beauty shop. But most of all, I loved the way she smelled, always wearing some fancy perfume. I would tell mom she ought to wear nice clothes and perfume like Mrs. Donnelly, but she would always say to me, "Now wouldn't that be plain silly and a waste to wear that stuff around the house?" Actually, I didn't think so. I loved to be around Mrs. Donnelly, and secretly, as much as I loved my mom, I used to wish she would be more like Mrs. Donnelly. Of course, as I got older, I realized that if she had tried to be more like someone else, she wouldn't have been the mom she was, the most important person in my life.

Sue had an older brother, Donny, and two younger sisters, Dru and Teri. And because her mom and dad were so active in the community and were always going out, babysitting was usually left to Sue. And because she was my best friend, I spent many, many nights at her house helping her watch her young sisters. We couldn't wait for them to go to bed. Then the fun would start. We'd put records on and spend the night giggling, eating, and talking about boys, of course. I learned to dance at her house. Together we'd practice the jitterbug, and I must say we got pretty good at it.

One Saturday night we were babysitting. It was probably about 11:00, when Sue decided she needed the back of her hair cut. "Hey, Linda, why don't you cut it for me," she said. "Are you kidding, I don't know how to cut hair." "Come on," she said, "It's not that hard. Just cut straight across." So I figured she was right. How hard could that be. I picked up the scissors and started cutting. Half way across, I realized it was looking mighty crooked. "Sue," I said, "this isn't turning out good." "Great, what am I going to do," she wailed. Well, immediately I knew what to do. Same as always when I needed help. I quickly picked up the phone and called mom, not even considering for a second that it was well after ll:00. I told her the problem and without hesitation she said she'd be right over. Ten minutes later there she was trying to salvage the mess I had made of Sue's hair. When she was done, she told us to have a good night and not do any more foolish things. In a flash she was gone, and it occurred to me how she didn't complain about coming out that time of night to help. Always unflappable.

One Halloween night, we were all trick-or-treating. Afterwards, we went back to Sue's house. She started talking about how she was mad at her next door neighbors and wouldn't it be fun to do something to their house. "They're out for the evening," she said. Next thing I know, there we were, Sue, Barb and I (and maybe a few others) all armed with a bar of soap. We went next door and started soaping their windows. Suddenly, the front door opens and there stands Sue's neighbor, very angry and yelling at us. Poor Sue, she got the worst of it. "Wait till I tell your parents what you did." We were all pretty scared. We said we were sorry and tore out of there as fast as we could. The next day, mom got a call from Mrs. Donnelly telling her what we did. "I want the girls to go over and wash it all off." Mom agreed. An hour later, there we were, washing windows. We never soaped another window.

Now and then, when mom was sewing some new clothes for me, she'd make a skirt for Sue. One summer, I think we were in seventh or eighth grade, I wanted her to make me a Bermuda skirt. She said okay. Then I asked her if she would make Sue one, too. That was fine with her and off we went to the store to get some fabric. I chose a light-weight corduroy in hot pink for myself and a bright turquoise for Sue. They were quite short, and had wide straps. Across the back, she connected the two straps with a horizontal piece of fabric. Then I had a great idea. "Hey, mom, why don't you cut out some letters and put our names on the back of the strap?" At first she didn't like the idea, but then agreed to it. When they were finished, I went over to Sue's and gave it to her. The next day we were going to meet and we decided we'd wear our new Bermuda skirts. We lived about a mile or so apart. We'd both leave our house at the same time and meet each other about half way. When we almost reached each other, two really cool looking guys in a convertible drove by. As they passed us, they hollered out "Hi, Sue... Hi, Linda." I can't tell you how excited we both were. We couldn't believe that two high school boys actually knew who we were. "Can you believe they know our names," we both cried. We were in 7th heaven and really thought we were cool. We continued our walk up town and when Sue turned around, I noticed her name on the back. Suddenly, it hit me. "Sue, our names are on the back. That's why those guys knew our names." We no longer felt cool, just dumb. We spent the rest of the day utterly depressed.

Barb had one of the sweetest moms. She was very soft-spoken and made everyone feel so welcome. We had a lot of pajama parties at her house. One of our favorite things to do, well after her parents had gone to bed, was to go out on their garage roof and sing and dance to a song called Captain Jinx. We had so much fun doing that, but looking back, how dumb we were. It would have been so easy to slip and go rolling right off the roof. But I guess that's what being a kid is—never worrying too much about anything. There's time enough for that. One day Sue and I were over at Barb's house upstairs in her bedroom. We thought we'd smoke a cigarette. We'd bought a pack earlier in the day, and started smoking them. None of us liked them but thought we looked so grown up doing it. After we'd been smoking for a while, her mom came upstairs to see what we were doing. When we heard her coming up the stairs we quickly put out the cigarettes. As she walked in the bedroom, I can still hear that soft, sweet voice of hers. "Girls, are you smoking?" We denied it vehemently, which is really a joke, considering her parents didn't smoke and the smell was overwhelming. But again, in her sweet way she just said, "Now girls, I don't want anymore smoking up here. If it happens again I'll have to tell your mothers." That was the end of that.

One afternoon Barb was over. We were sitting outside deciding what we should do. For some reason I mentioned that our neighbors, the Brandy's, weren't home. They had a small home on a lake in Indiana and during the summer, they spent almost all their time up there. I was describing to Barb what their house looked like inside, and suddenly we had an idea. We decided we'd break in since no one was home — just to look around. We tried all the doors and windows, and finally found a window that was unlocked. We raised the window and climbed inside. Once inside, we took just a few steps, and suddenly realized the enormity of what we had just done. "What if they decide to come back early," Barb said. "I'll get killed, that's for sure," I said. We panicked. Almost simultaneously we cried, "Let's get out of here quick!" With that we scrambled back out the window, closed it quickly and fled back to my yard in record time. Even after being safely in my yard, we both kept looking around to see if anyone had seen us. Thankfully, no one had. The stupid things kids can do just for kicks.

Judy Porter perhaps had the most intellectual family. Her father was president of Markham. I didn't know him all that well because he was rarely around when we were over there. Guess he was tending to town business, but I thought it pretty neat to be a friend of the town president. Mrs. Porter was a very classy and intelligent lady, the only one of our mother's who had a college education, which I also found very impressive. They had a nice home with the largest family room I ever saw in my life. When Judy would have pajama parties, it was heaven. All that room to dance around in. No matter how much noise we made, her mom never yelled and told us to be quiet. Along side of her house was a large hill, and in the winter, a bunch of us would go sledding down it. One winter Sue brought a toboggan and we all piled on it. There were lots of trees on the hillside and one time we tried to swerve but it didn't work. We slammed into the tree hurting the first guy in front. Bruce was his name, and thankfully, he wasn't hurt too bad. But it sure did scare us.

Donna Olson was the prettiest of all of us. Thankfully, she was just as nice, too, so we didn't mind the fact she was beautiful. She had a smile that lit up a room, and a laugh that was infectious. We were not only friends, but because she had a crush on Tommy, she came over a lot, hoping he would be there. She did the darndest things too. One time she was spending the night. I only had a twin bed in my room so when friends stayed over, it was kind of cramped with two of us in bed, but we didn't mind. After talking and laughing ourselves silly, we finally turned in for the night. As we lay in the bed we continued to chat. Suddenly Donna turned to me and said, "Hey, Linda, I don't feel…" That's as far as she got. Next thing I knew she was throwing up all over me and the bed. It was really gross. Not knowing what to do, I did what I always did in a crisis. "Mom," I shrieked. "Come quick." Seconds later mom came running upstairs into the room, turned on the light and asked "What's wrong?" But just as quickly, she could see what was wrong. Calmly, she asked Donna if she felt okay, and when Donna reassured her that she did, mom then told us to get out of bed, she handed Donna a pair of my pj's, to change into, and proceeded to change the bedding. In a matter of minutes, everything was back to normal, Donna and I were once again back in bed, and mom was down stairs doing a quick load of laundry. The following morning, other than asking

Donna how she felt, the incident was never brought up again (except by me, 45 years later)!

When I was in eighth grade, our teacher called Sue, Barb, Donna, Judy and me into her classroom and said she was forming a singing group and wanted the five of us to be in it. She ended up asking two other girls, Judy Pagan, and Sharon Kennedy to join the group. We would be called Teen Toppers. We practiced after school under her direction, singing a song called "Mr. Sandman." I'd like to say we sounded great, but we didn't. We sang off-key and were flat, but I'm not sure we cared. It was lots of fun, and she said that when we got better, we could sing at school dances. Then one day when we met for practice, she said we couldn't do this any more. Apparently, a number of other students were very upset they couldn't be in the group. They didn't think it was fair and complained to the principal. The principal, in turn, told our teacher to dismantle the group. She didn't have a choice, but suggested that, if we really enjoyed it, we should meet away from the school, and get rid of the name Teen Toppers. And because she played the piano for us, we would have to find a piano player. We all decided we'd give it a try on our own. We invited a girl named Donna Bonaker, who played the piano, to join our group, and we became The Harmonettes. The Harmonettes weren't any better than the Teen Toppers, in fact, probably worse, not having a teacher to guide us. Nevertheless, we practiced, and at our 8th grade graduation dance, the school let us sing. We sang, what else, "Graduation

Day." We were really nervous getting up on the stage and singing in front of all our classmates, but we managed to do it without any major gaffs, other than singing off-key. That was our first and last public performance. After that night, we gave up on the group. Summer was here, and then we'd be starting high school in the fall.

Each year the eighth grade class at Markham Park would take a trip to Springfield, the capital of Illinois. They would tour the capitol, visit Lincoln's log cabin, and in general, get a lesson in government. This trip was the highlight for eighth graders. Arriving at the school at 6:00 AM, several Greyhound buses would be waiting to drive the students the approximately 185 miles to Springfield. The three hour drive was fun. Everyone was laughing, talking, singing silly songs, and having a great time. At the end of the day, and before starting the long trip home, the class would stop at a fancy restaurant for supper. The dinners had been ordered and paid for in advance. I was really looking forward to that, never having been in a really nice restaurant before. The times we did eat out, it was usually at the counter of Woolworths, or Art's Pizza, and occasionally at McDonalds.

Arriving at the restaurant, everyone was seated, and busy discussing the days events while they waited for their food. Several waitresses appeared carrying trays loaded with salads. As I watched them place the salads at the table next to ours, I couldn't figure out why they were serving them first. All my life we ate our salad after the main meal was served. So did our relatives. I just assumed that's how everyone did it. No one else seemed to be noticing this strange occurrence. I finally asked Sue, who was sitting next to me, why they were serving the salad now. She looked at me strangely, and mumbled something about they were serving it because it was time to eat. When the waitress finally got to our table and placed a salad in front of me, once again I was shocked. All over the salad was something orange. Again, I turned to Sue and asked what on earth was on our salad, and for the second time, she looked at me strangely. She said it was French dressing. I had never seen French dressing before, or even heard of it. The only thing we ever had on a salad at home or at a relative's house was vinegar and oil. I was afraid to even taste it, but since everyone else seemed to be enjoying theirs, I took a bite. I thought it was absolutely gross. "Is this what the French really eat," I thought. I remember fearfully wondering what the rest of the meal would be like, and if there were any other surprises in store for me. And since I can't recall what the remainder of the meal consisted of, I can only assume I enjoyed it.

When we finally arrived back at the school late at night, tired but happy, mom was waiting. When I got in the car, the first thing I told her about was the strange salad. She said she knew that restaurants served the salads first but was sure people didn't do that in their own homes. As for the French dressing, she agreed with me. She said she had it one time when she and dad were out, and thought it gross, too.

It's Elementary

When I finally started school, I was so excited. Tommy had started the year before me. One would think that I would have loved those days to myself with just my mom, but fact is, I missed him terribly, mean tricks and all. I'd wait all day for him to come home. When I saw the school bus approaching, I'd run out to the end of the street to meet him. He'd always have some great story to tell. Most of all, though, he was learning to read and write and that's something I wanted to do so bad. I'd look through all his books with such excitement. My favorite was his "Dick and Jane" book. Finally, my first day of school arrived. The week before, mom had taken us shopping for new school clothes and supplies, as she did every year thereafter. We would drive all the way to Hammond, Indiana where we'd spend an entire day shopping, and mid day we'd stop for lunch. Having lunch out was really a big deal to us since we rarely did so. We'd usually sit at the counter of a Woolworth's or some similar store and get a hamburger and coke. Then we'd continue shopping.

We'd go home late in the day with a car full of new things. I could hardly wait to wear them, but mom said we couldn't touch any of it until school started. We always had a big picnic on Labor Day that we all looked forward to, but this year I was just anxious for it to end so I could get up and go to school. My first grade teacher was Mrs. Sauerbauer, and her name sort of fit her. She was a good teacher, but a no-nonsense type. She sort of scared me. School had been in session about a month when one afternoon Mrs. Sauerbauer said if anyone had to use the bathroom, they could get up and go now. The girls' bathroom had five stalls. The middle stall had a large crack in the seat. Every time I sat on it, it pinched terribly. After several bad pinches, I made sure I never used the middle stall again. Leaving the classroom, I followed other girls to the bathroom. All the stalls were taken except that dreaded middle stall. I stood there waiting for another stall to be vacant. Mrs. Sauerbauer suddenly appeared. "Linda," she yelled. "Why are you just standing there? Get back to class." I started to explain about the cracked seat, but she didn't seem to care. "Leave, right now," she said again. "But I really have to go." "Too bad," she said. "There's an empty stall and you didn't use it." With that, she gave me a smack on my behind and nearly pushed me out the door. I spent the rest of the afternoon squirming in my seat and thinking that maybe it was more fun to stay home.

Aside from my initial dislike of my first grade teacher, I loved school. I made lots of friends, and enjoyed learning. I also loved having Tommy at my school. The years went by quickly, though, and Tommy was about to go to a new school. Today they would call it "middle school"

"The new school is great, just great!" Tommy was telling everyone as soon as they sat down for supper. Today had been the first day of school, and Tommy, a sixth grader now, went to the new Markham Park junior high school on the other side of town, while Linda, in the fifth grade, still attended the old McLaughry elementary school.

"What's so great about it?" Linda wanted to know. She liked McLaughry. All of her friends went to McLaughry, and she also liked her new teacher, Mrs. Jacobs—although the very first thing Mrs. Jacobs said to her was that she thought she should be wearing eyeglasses. Had she caught her squinting at the blackboard?

"You'll just have to wait a year to find out," Tommy told her. "But take my word for it, it's got McLaughry beat hands down. You should see the gym. It's huge. Even the bathrooms are great."

"Do you like Miss Winkler?" mom asked.

"She's great, just great," Tommy said. "Especially after Mrs. Stone last year." Mrs. Stone, Tommy's fifth grade teacher, had often told the class she didn't know why she put up with them, when she could make more money working in an office in downtown

Chicago. Mrs. Stone hated kids, and all the kids knew it.

Linda was sick of hearing Tommy rave about Markham Park. Ever since he got home from school he'd gone on and on — about how the school smelled so new, about how cool all the older kids are. He told her he never liked the name McLaughry — how much cooler the name Markham Park, especially the "Park" part.

Dad cut off another large chunk of the meat loaf. "Very good, Betty, he said, pouring himself more wine. "I hope you made enough."

"There's another pan keeping warm in the oven, don't worry," mom said. "You even have enough for sandwiches in your lunches tomorrow —"

"Hey dad," Tommy interrupted. "Markham Park is starting a basketball team and I'm going out for it. So is Jackie Baker and Jim Mannaioni and Bobby Livingston. The coach, Mr. McGovern, came to our classroom today and said tryouts would be in two weeks. Do you think we could get a basketball hoop in the driveway?"

"Ask your mother," dad said. "She has the checkbook."

Mom dismissed dad's words with a wave of her arm. "We'll go down to Goldblatts on Saturday and see if they have basketball hoops," she said. "I bet that's where the Livingston's got theirs."

Linda said, "Maybe you should just use the Livingston's basketball hoop to practice until you find out if you like it first."

"Now this girl's got a head on her shoulders," dad said.

"People who go to a school named McLaughry that doesn't even have a basketball team don't have a voice in the matter," Tommy says.

A few days later, Linda's, fifth grade teacher, Mrs. Jacobs, stops her after class one day. "Linda, you seem to be having trouble seeing the blackboard. I think you may need glasses," she says.

"No, I can see okay."

"Linda, you know that's not true. Tomorrow, I'm going to move you to the front row. That should help. In the meantime, please take this note home to your parents." She hands Linda an envelope.

Linda was dying to see exactly what Mrs. Jacob's had written, but the envelope was sealed. She briefly debates whether to open it, but then thinks better of it. Arriving at home, after a quick hello to mom, she hurries up to her room. She places the envelope on her desk under a pile of papers. She figures it can wait a while. Upset over this turn of events, she plops down on her bed and sulks.

Tommy, just getting home from school, comes upstairs, and seeing her sitting on her bed, looking forlorn, asks her what's wrong.

"I have a note from Mrs. Jacobs for mom and dad."

"Linda's in trouble," he taunts. "What'd you do wrong?"

"I didn't do anything wrong, and I'm not in trouble," she

quickly said. *"I think she's telling them I need glasses."*

"Well, you do practically sit on top the TV every night in order to see, and you're constantly squinting. Maybe you do need glasses. You better give them the note. See ya later, four eyes."

Four eyes! That's what was really bothering Linda. No one else in her class wore glasses and she was afraid everyone would make fun of her... like Tommy just did.

Doris has just come over to ask if Linda would like to walk up town with her. She has to get some milk for her mom. Linda gladly goes with her. It will take her mind off the note, at least for now. She'll worry about it later.

She gets back just in time for supper. Mom has made one of their favorite meals, stew and polenta, and is just putting it on the table. Linda was sorry she hadn't been home to help her make it. It was a big production for mom. She would make the stew earlier in the day. Then shortly before it was time to eat, she'd fill this enormous pot with water, add a little salt, and wait for it to come to a full boil. Once boiling, she would slowly pour the dry corn meal in and begin stirring. Because the pot was so large, a regular spoon was way too small. Years earlier, when she first started making polenta, she had told dad her problem with the spoon. He quickly solved the problem. He took an old broom stick handle, cut about a foot off the end, scrubbed it clean, and gave it to mom. It worked perfectly. She's been using it ever since. The polenta had to be stirred constantly or it would burn. Linda loved to help with the stirring, and now and then mom would let her. As the corn meal thickened, it became harder and harder to stir. It would get all bubbly and the bubbles sometimes would burst, splattering all over. That's when mom would take over. She didn't want Linda getting burnt like she had on so many occasions.

"Hey, Linda," Tommy says as she enters the breakfast nook. "Look what mom made. I can't wait to dig in."

Linda doesn't reply. The note was on her mind again.

While filling all our plates, dad says, "It's too bad grandma isn't here. She loves polenta. I'm surprised you didn't wait to make it until she gets back." Grandma has gone to Aunt Dee's for a visit and won't be back for two weeks.

"Well, I thought of that, too, but stew meat was the only meat I had in the freezer. Saturday I'll have to go into Harvey and stop at Shinner's Meat Market. I'll make polenta again when grandma gets back. Kids, you won't mind if I make it again in a few weeks, will you?" mom asks.

"Are you kidding?" Tommy says. "You can make it every day if you want."

Linda doesn't reply.

"Tom," Betty says. "Mr. Schmadeke stopped by today. He asked if I'd be an election judge at our polling place next week." Mr. Schmadeke lives on the next block. We rarely see him except around election time. He works for the state and always says keeping his job depends on the outcome of the election. He was also in charge of getting people to work at the polls.

"Well, what did you tell him?"

"I told him I'd check with you and let him know in a few days," mom says.

"I think you should do it. Besides doing your civic duty, it will be good for you to get out of the house a little," dad says.

Tommy puts his two cents in, "I think you should do it too, mom."

"I'm just not sure. I'd be gone from 8 AM until 8 PM."

"So.... what's the problem?" dad asks.

"The problem is that the kids would be home alone for over two hours until you get home from work. Now if grandma were here there'd be no problem."

"Geez, mom," Tommy says. "I'm 12 and Linda's 10. We can certainly stay alone for a couple hours."

"Tommy's right. They're old enough," dad says.

"Well maybe they are, but what about supper?"

"Betty, you worry too much. I can make supper. We're not completely helpless, although I'm sure the meal won't be nearly as good as one of your meals. We'll survive though. Right, kids?"

"Right, dad," Tommy says, and again, no response from Linda.

"Linda, you're awfully quiet tonight. Do you feel all right?" mom asks.

Linda is usually the chatterbox at dinner, constantly going on and on about everything that happened at school and after school, usually interrupting anyone else who is talking.

"I'm fine, mom."

Tommy blurts out, "She got a note from Mrs. Jacobs today to give to you and dad." Linda glares at him angrily.

"What note? I haven't seen any note. Where's the note, Linda?"

"It's in my room. I'll get it after supper."

"No, you'll get it right now. Bring it to me. Right now!"

Linda leaves the table, goes upstairs and returns with the note in hand. Reluctantly, she hands it to mom, who promptly tears open the envelope and begins to read.

"What does it say, Betty?" dad asks.

"Mrs. Jacobs says Linda is having a hard time seeing the blackboard. She thinks we should get her eyes examined. I'll make an appointment first thing tomorrow with Dr. Snyder. Grandma goes to him and she likes him."

"Mom, please," Linda says. "I don't want glasses."

"Why on earth wouldn't you want to see better?"

Dad says, "There's nothing wrong with wearing glasses. Your grandma wears them."

"Yeah, but she's old."

"Well, I use them for reading. You going to tell me I'm old, too?" dad replies.

Linda says nothing.

"She's afraid everyone will make fun of her," Tommy says.

"Yeah, just like you did, " Linda says.

"Tommy, what did you say to your sister?" dad asks.

Linda interjects, "He called me four eyes."

"I was just teasing her, dad."

"Well, no more teasing. Do you understand?"

"What's the big deal about glasses anyway?" Tommy counters.

Mom finally says, "There will be no more name calling. Linda, if you need glasses, you're going to get them. Period. Now let's finish supper."

Later that night in her room, Tommy stops by to chat.

"Get out of my room."

"What's the matter with you?"

"You know what's wrong. You had to mention the note."

"Oh for Heavens sake, Linda. You know what's wrong with you? You always think everything I do is mean. Let me tell you something. I actually did you a favor. You weren't going to give them the note today. Then you would have spent the whole night tossing and turning and fretting about it. And tomorrow morning you would have been scared to go to class knowing Mrs. Jacobs would ask you about the note. Now, thanks to me, you can sleep peacefully tonight and tomorrow when you see Mrs. Jacobs, you'll be able to tell her you gave them the note. Now, where's my thank you?"

Linda wouldn't admit it to Tommy, but she knew he was right. He did do her a big favor by telling them.

Sure enough, the next day when she entered the classroom, the first thing Mrs. Jacobs did was ask Linda what her parents said.

"Mom said she's going to make an appointment with an eye doctor," Linda quietly says, and retreats quickly to her desk, now in the first row.

Two days later, Linda is sitting in Dr. Snyder's office. He has just finished examining her eyes and is telling mom that she definitely needs glasses.

"They should be ready in about a week," Dr. Snyder says. I'll give you a call when they come in. Now lets pick out a frame for you."

A week later Linda walks out of Dr. Snyder's office with her new glasses. She can't believe how good she can see. Everything looks so big and beautiful. On the ride home, she can't stop looking out the window, reading signs she could never see before. She loves her new glasses.

Before taking Linda to the doctor that afternoon, mom had given Tommy a final warning. "Linda is going to be very self conscious. I don't want any teasing whatsoever from you. Do I make my self clear?

"Yeah, mom, but I still don't see what the big deal is."

"The big deal is that she doesn't want to be different. At her age, especially for girls, fitting in is very important. She'll be the only one in her class wearing glasses. I understand how she feels. Dad and I talked it over, and if you do any teasing, your punishment is going to be severe. You won't be allowed to go to the Friday night square dances at your school for the next two months. We mean it, Tommy."

"OK, I'll be nice."

When they arrive home, true to his word, Tommy doesn't tease her. He actually tells her that she looks very nice in them. That night watching television, Linda can see the TV without sitting on the floor right in front of it. And later that night in her room, she is able to read her new Nancy Drew book without squinting. She falls asleep thinking that she should have gotten glasses years before.

The next morning, as they are leaving for school, mom hands Linda her glasses, just cleaned spotless. She puts them on and mom tells her how nice she looks. Linda and Tommy walk toward the bus stop. When she is safely out of mom's sight, she removes the glasses and puts them in her pocket.

"What are you doing, Linda? Tommy asks, somewhat surprised. "I thought you said you love your glasses."

"I do...at home. I'm not wearing them in school."

"I'm telling mom tonight."

"Please, Tommy. Don't. I'm begging you." Tears were starting to well up in her eyes. "Just give me some time. Please!"

Linda looked so pathetic that he suddenly felt sorry for her. "Okay, your secret is safe with me. I won't say anything, but I think you're nuts for not wearing them."

Several weeks passed, and Linda followed the same routine

each day. She'd put the glasses on before leaving the house, take them off before getting on the bus, then put them back on when she got off the bus each afternoon. Mom and dad would ask how she was doing in school with the glasses and Linda would always say okay. Surprisingly, Tommy didn't say anything. From time to time he would try to blackmail her by telling her if she didn't do what he wanted, he would tell. At times, she wondered how long she could keep up this deceit.

One afternoon, after getting off the bus and putting the glasses on, she runs gingerly into the house, all anxious to tell mom about the days activities. Mom was waiting at the door.

"How was school today, Linda?"

"Good. Can I go with Sue..."

Mom cut her off. "Mrs. Jacobs called me today. Do you know what she wanted?" Linda says nothing. "Well, I'll tell you. She wanted to know when I'm going to take you for an eye examination because she really says you're having a hard time reading. She also said she can't believe that we're taking our slow sweet time about this."

Linda looks away, unable to look mom in the eye. Just then Tommy walks in the door.

"Tommy, did you know your sister is not wearing her glasses in school?"

He hesitates for a brief moment. "Yes," he says.

"Why didn't you tell me?"

"I promised Linda I wouldn't."

"Well, that's nice. You pick on her all the time, and the one time you should have spoken up, you didn't." She was really angry with him.

"Mom, please, it's not his fault. I begged him not to say anything, and for once, he did what I asked."

"Your dad is not going to be happy about this. Tomorrow you will wear your glasses in school."

The next morning she leaves the house wearing her glasses. Approaching the bus stop, Linda once again removes them. Tommy can't believe it.

"Are you crazy? You're really going to get in trouble, and this time I'm not going to cover for you."

"Leave me alone," she says and gets on the bus.

When she walks in the classroom, glasses in her pocket, Mrs. Jacobs is waiting for her. Linda's heart starts to pound.

"Linda, isn't there something you want to do before you take your seat?" She reaches into Linda's pocket, removes the glasses and hands them to her. "Now put them on." She gives Linda's hand a gentle squeeze. "It's going to be okay."

A few kids make a comment or two, but for the most part, everyone is pretty nice. Mainly they keep asking her what it was like to wear glasses. In a matter of days, the glasses were no longer a topic of conversation. Linda would think about the agony she put herself through. How many times she could recall dad saying, "Tell the truth and be honest. Life is much more simple that way." AMEN!

Two weeks have passed. Tommy and Linda are excited. Tomorrow, when they come home from school, mom won't be there. That's all they've talked about for the past week. Tomorrow is election day and mom has agreed to work at the polls. Never, in all their years of school, have they ever come home to an empty house. Mom is almost always there, and if on a rare occasion she isn't, then grandma is. But grandma has decided to stay one more week at Aunt Dee's and won't be home until the weekend.

Supper is over, and they are sitting in Linda's room listening to records and talking about tomorrow.

"What will we do tomorrow after school?" Linda asks.

"Anything! Anything we want! Won't that be fun," Tommy says. "I can hardly wait."

"Me, too," Linda agrees, but she's not sure if she's quite as excited as Tommy. She's never been alone in her life. The thought that tomorrow she and Tommy will be on their own is both exciting and a bit daunting.

"One thing we'll do for sure is go out on the roof for a few minutes," Tommy says. "At least we won't have to worry that mom will catch us."

Meanwhile, downstairs, mom is washing dishes, and cooking. Dad walks into the kitchen.

"Betty, what are you cooking?"

"Oh, I'm making some spaghetti sauce for your dinner tomorrow night. All you'll have to do is reheat it. You always say

you think reheated spaghetti tastes as good, if not better, the second day."

"That's true, but you don't have to do that. I can fix something for the kids and myself."

"I know you can, Tom, but you work hard all day. You shouldn't have to come home and cook your own supper."

"Betty, you work hard all day, too. Don't think I don't know that."

"Well, the sauce is almost done. I'm also going to make a salad. I'll keep it covered in the refrigerator. All you have to do is add some vinegar and oil. There's a fresh loaf of Gonnella bread in the bread box, and there is still half an apple pie left for dessert. And don't worry about the dishes. I'll wash them when I get home."

"Betty, you spoil us."

Looking a little flustered, mom shrugs him off with a wave of her hand. "No I don't. It's my job to take care of all of you, and I enjoy it. You know that.

"Yes, I do, Betty." With that, dad retreats to the front room to watch some TV, leaving mom to finish up in the kitchen.

The next morning, Tommy and Linda are getting ready for school. Before they leave, mom gives them last minute instructions.

"Tommy, the key will be under the porch mat. Make sure you both do your homework if you have any. Don't be mean to Linda. If you have any problems, call Mrs. Walker. She knows you're *going to be home alone. I've put her phone number by the telephone. No friends in the house, and don't leave the yard. Absolutely no going out on the roof. Don't forget...*

"Geez, mom," Tommy interrupts. *"We're only going to be alone for two and a half hours. You act like you're going away for a week."*

"Now don't get smart. I just don't want to worry about you two. Just do as I say. Linda, behave yourself. Tommy, no fighting."

"Bye, mom," they both say and hurry out the door before she can think of more things to say.

School passes quickly, and now they are unlocking the door to get in. The house seems so quiet when they walk inside, and strange not to have mom there greeting them. They quickly kick off their shoes and throw their jackets on the floor, something mom would never allow. They start running through the house yelling at the top of their lungs. Then they start jumping up and down on mom's and dad's bed.

"Let's get something to eat," Linda says. They find some cupcakes and pour themselves a glass of milk. "What should we do next?"

"Lets shoot some baskets," Tommy says. "Then if you want, I'll play hopscotch with you."

They do both, without a whole lot enthusiasm.

"Want to go for a bike ride?"

"No," Tommy says. "I really don't feel like it. Besides, I

think mom wants us to stay here. I know, lets go out on the roof. We always have fun up there."

"Okay. Last one on the roof is a rotten egg." Out on the roof, they run up and down for a few minutes. Then come back inside.

"Let's watch some television," Tommy says. "I think Uncle Mistletoe is on. You like that show."

After watching television for a few minutes, Linda asks what time it is.

"4:00," Tommy says. "We've got almost an hour and a half yet till dad gets home. Isn't this fun?"

"Yeah, loads." Linda wasn't having all that good a time. She wouldn't tell Tommy, but she missed having her mom there. Somehow she wasn't having as much fun as she thought she would.

"I know, Linda, let's put on the boxing gloves and spar a little."

"Are you kidding? You pound me enough when mom's here. I don't even want to think how hard you'll hit me without her here."

Tommy, looking rather serious, says, "Actually, Linda, you're wrong. Whether you believe me or not, I'd never hurt you when we're alone like this."

For some reason, she believed him, and they put on the gloves. After a few minutes of sparring lightly, and no hard punches thrown by Tommy, they tire of that quickly, too.

"Now what," Linda asks.

"Well, we could play ping pong. Or maybe checkers. Whatever you want."

They play some checkers, then Linda says, "Let's climb the tree."

"Okay," Tommy says, and they go outside.

"What time is it now, Tommy?"

He checks his watch. "4:30." An hour to go yet, he thought.

"Is that all it is?" This day sure wasn't going like they thought it would.

After climbing down from the tree, Linda says to Tommy, "I know you're going to say I'm a baby, but I'm not having that much fun. I miss mom. I wish she were here."

"So do I. For some reason, we built up in our minds how great it would be to have the house to ourselves. But it isn't that much fun. Let's go watch TV again."

Heading back into the house, Tommy says, "Hey, Linda, let's put our shoes away and hang up our jackets. No need for mom to see them laying on the floor."

After watching TV again, they get out a deck of cards. They are playing War, when they hear dad's car pull in the driveway. They both go flying out the door to greet him.

"Hi kids. How's everything going? Did you have fun by yourselves?"

"Yeah, great, dad, we're having fun, aren't we Linda?"

"Sure are. Wish we could do it more often."

Dad gives them each a half stick of spearmint gum and reminds them to save it for after supper.

"Let me get out of this suit, and then I'll get supper ready."

"I'll help you, dad," Linda says.

"So will I," says Tommy.

After dad changes clothes, the three of them go into the kitchen. Tommy and Linda set the table, while dad starts reheating the spaghetti. They fix the salad, dad slices the Gonnella bread, and they sit down to eat. They make small chitchat, but for the most part, they are all more quiet than usual. When supper is over, dad starts to clean the kitchen.

"Your mom said to leave the dishes for her, but I think it would be nice if we cleaned up for her. You kids can help."

"Okay," Tommy says. "Linda, you can wash and I'll dry." Dad clears the table and puts things away while Linda and Tommy do the dishes. When the kitchen is clean, they go into the front room. Dad heads for the piano and Tommy and Linda follow. Dad plays while they sing, and about 10 minutes into it, dad gets up and says he's tired. They'll play more tomorrow night.

The three of them settle in front of the TV, each one barely concentrating on what they are watching. The evening, which usually goes by so fast, seems to be going so slow tonight. Several times Tommy and Linda see dad look at his watch.

Finally, they hear a car pull in the driveway and know it must be mom. All three of them are at the door when she walks in.

"Hi, mom," Linda says, giving her a big hug.

"Hi kids, Hi Tom." "How'd everything go after school?"

"Oh, we had a great time," Tommy says.

"Yeah, the best," Linda adds.

The house suddenly has come alive. They start talking up a storm, each one trying to be heard over the other. Dad finally says, "Hey, kids, why don't you go play for a while. Let your mom have a little quiet. She must be tired. Betty, I made a pot of coffee. I thought maybe you'd enjoy a cup." He puts his arm around her shoulder and they walk into the kitchen, as Tommy and Linda watch with surprised looks on their faces.

Seconds later, Tommy and Linda go charging up the stairs talking and laughing, and then Linda lets out a loud yell, as Tommy deliberately trips her on a stair.

"I'm telling mom you tripped me," Linda hollers.

"Oh, quit being a baby. I didn't mean it. You got in the way of my foot. It's your fault."

Downstairs, mom comments on the spotless kitchen as she pours them each a cup of coffee. And she hears the kids upstairs arguing about something. "Well, I see everything went okay. I thought maybe everyone would miss me, at least a little."

"We all missed you, Betty, believe me, we all did."

God's in His Heaven (mom's in her kitchen)...all's right with the world!

HAPPY DAYS

Hot, lazy summers, balmy fall days, cold, snowy winters, glorious springtime — the changing seasons were always looked forward to with new excitement of things to come. And as much as one might complain about the excessive heat and humidity, or the frigid temperatures, I wouldn't trade any of the seasons. It's what keeps life interesting.

Summer was probably my favorite season growing up. For starters, no school for three whole months. Running out of school that final day in June was exciting knowing all the fun that was in store for us. In addition to going up to Honey Lake, and dad's vacation, summer also brought an abundance of other fun. Summer days would find most of the neighborhood kids at our house, where we would play until well after dark. Baseball was a big favorite. On the vacant lot next to our house, we had plenty of room to knock a ball "out of the park." Hide and seek was another favorite, especially after dark. Of course, Tommy would always find some way to scare the daylights out of me. The neighboring town of Harvey had a public swimming pool. Many days Tommy, Kerry and I would take the bus into Harvey and spend the entire day at the pool, coming home in late afternoon totally exhausted, but thoroughly refreshed. The only drawback was those darn geese we had to encounter on our walk to and from the bus stop. We learned to swim at the pool so by the time we started going to Honey Lake we were able to swim well enough to get out to the raft.

St. Christopher Church, in the neighboring town of Midlothian, had an annual carnival. On Saturday and Sunday afternoons, mom would give Tommy and me each five dollars and we'd spend both days going on rides, stuffing ourselves with food, and hanging around with our friends. It was an event we looked forward to each year. One of the major attractions of the carnival was the raffling of a new car on the final night of the carnival. The car to be raffled was always the same…a big, beautiful Cadillac. Mom would buy a book of tickets, and just before the drawing each year, I'd get so excited just thinking that maybe, just maybe, we would win. I'd imagine them calling out our name, and then handing us the keys to the new car. And I'd imagine riding around town, and having mom pick up my friends, no longer embarrassed by showing up in the Nash. Dad would surely get rid of it if we won, wouldn't he?

The 4th of July was eagerly looked forward to each year. During the day, we'd hang around the house. Sometimes company would come over. But whether anyone else came or not, mom always made a picnic type of meal — fried chicken and potato salad, finishing the meal with watermelon. At night, after dark, we would go to the fireworks celebration in town, and when we got home, dad would give Tommy and me each a few boxes of sparklers and we'd go out in the front yard and light them until they were all gone. It was a day we always looked forward to. After Carol Hayward's death, though, the 4th of July would never be the same for me.

As summer neared to an end, and dad's vacation was over, it was time for another school year to begin. As we settled into a new school year, fall was rapidly approaching, and with it, another season for us to enjoy. The leaves from our many trees made a playground of fun for us. We could play endlessly with them. Leaf burning was legal back then, and we always set aside a Saturday afternoon for burning them. We worked hard raking all those leaves, and it wasn't much fun, except for grandma — she loved raking them. After a long day of raking, and watching them burn, dad would gather up small branches and build a small bonfire for us. Mom would supply the hot dogs and marshmallows, plus chips and soft drinks. We would spend several hours singing by the campfire and roasting our hotdogs and marshmallows. Sometimes she'd let my friend Doris join us. I loved the smell of burning leaves, and all these years later, if I'm out in the country and see burning leaves, I immediately open the car windows and let the pungent smell fill the car, my mind drifting back to those days long ago.

Halloween was a big occasion I really looked forward to. Not only did mom make us great costumes that were so much fun to wear, but it was also my birthday — a double treat. The week before Halloween, mom would buy a large pumpkin. It was dad's job to carve it, and it was something he enjoyed doing. After supper, when the kitchen was cleaned, he'd sit at the table and spend the evening carving the pumpkin. And when the pumpkin was carved to his satisfaction, mom would gather up all the pumpkin seeds and wash them. She'd then place them on a cookie sheet, sprinkle on some salt, and then roast them in the oven until they were completely dry. Dad loved pumpkin seeds and would spend the next few evenings snacking on them.

After supper was finished, mom would bring out my birthday cake. They would all sing "Happy Birthday" to me and I would open my presents. While this was all fun, truth is, all Tommy and I really wanted was to get started with our trick-or-treating. It would be dark by then, and often quite chilly, and along with friends, off we'd go. We'd stay out sometimes till midnight, and come home with a shopping bag packed full of scrumptious candies. Mom would always be waiting up for us, never worried about the lateness, and never having to warn us beforehand not to eat anything until she inspected it. Most of the time we'd come home stuffed from having eaten so much of it already.

As fall succumbed to winter, we looked forward to Thanksgiving. Dinner was always at our house, with mom's relatives, and she cooked up a feast. The week proceeding she would be busy baking pies, usually several pumpkin pies, plus a raisin or coconut for dad. Waking up on Thanksgiving morning, the house was already filled with wonderful smells. The turkey was in the oven, and it seemed as though the morning would never end. We were so anxious for everyone to arrive. As usual, after we ate, dad would play the piano for everyone.

After Thanksgiving, the next month would be filled with the excitement of Christmas — and two weeks off from school. By now, winter was in full swing and what a glorious season it was. At the first sight of snow, Tommy and I would be outside building snowmen and making snow angels. Sometimes he would talk me into a snowball fight. "Come on, Linda, it'll be fun," he'd say. "I promise I won't hit you hard." Yeah, right. Why did I always believe him? He'd start out throwing soft ones, as promised, but gradually he'd start hurling them until one would really smack me hard in the face. That would be the end of snowballs — until the next snowfall, when again he'd promise to throw gently. I'd believe him, and of course, he would end up hurling another whopper and that would end another session of snowballs. And on and on it went like that, all winter.

One year it was decided that Janice would spend the week between Christmas and New Years at our house. On Christmas Day, after an early supper, Aunt Di and Uncle George left for home, leaving a very excited Janice with us. She'd never been away from home before and was looking forward to it. That evening we went to bed fairly early because we were all tired from the busy couple of days we had. The next morning, bright and early, Janice jumped out of bed all eager to begin what she thought would be a fun week. We had a heavy snowfall the day before leaving at least five inches of snow on the ground, and Janice couldn't wait to go outside and build a snowman with Tommy and me. Grandma was planning to take all of us to a movie one day during the week, and mom had said that on another day we'd take the train downtown to see the Christmas decorations and then have lunch.

When Janice came downstairs for breakfast, mom noticed that she was flushed and didn't look well. Of course, Janice insisted she was fine. But by the time breakfast was finished, we all knew she wasn't. She had the measles! That poor girl was covered from head to toe with them. I felt so sorry for her. That evening, when Aunt Di got home from work, mom called to tell her about Janice. Aunt Di said they would come out and get her in the morning, but Mom said she didn't mind keeping Janice with us, assuring her we would all take good care of her. Aunt Di agreed. It was a long week. Instead of playing with the new things we got for Christmas, and going outside to play in the snow and build a snowman, there we sat in the house with a sad and sick cousin. There would be no movie or train ride downtown, either. Tommy and I did our best to cheer her up, playing games with her and just keeping her company. This sure wasn't how she had envisioned the week, but despite the measles, she was a real trouper. She never complained and I think, all things considered, she still enjoyed her stay with us. By the following weekend, she was beginning to feel better, just in time to go home. She learned at a very early age that sometimes the best laid plans don't always work out. Meanwhile, Tommy and I, never having had the measles, worried that we'd come down with them next. Fortunately, we didn't.

The year we got the sleds for Christmas was one of the best winters. Our street, having nothing but some gravel, would freeze to a sheet of ice. We'd run up and down the street doing belly flops. It still amazes me how long we would stay outdoors in freezing temperatures, never complaining about how cold it was, or tiring. It was just so much fun. And when we finally did go inside, mom would always have hot chocolate waiting to warm us up.

Beyond the ditch at the back of our property where we used to build our villages was an open field that stretched for several acres. In the center of that open field was a low spot that would collect water, and after several nights of freezing temperatures, the field would turn into a wonderful ice rink. Tommy and I would walk about 10 minutes to reach this ice pond, and we'd just have fun sliding around on it. Sometimes we'd drag our sleds with us and do belly flops on it. We'd always come home and tell mom how much fun it was. One Christmas, Tommy and I both got ice skates. Then the fun really began. During our two-week break from school, we would go out to the pond and skate for hours. By the end of the day, we would be so cold we could hardly walk back home. More than once, I thought I wouldn't make it. My feet were numb. Tommy would keep after me to keep walking. "Just a little further, Linda. You can make it." "No, I can't," I'd moan. These were the times he'd actually be nice, offering to carry my skates for me and reminding me that when we walked in the door, mom would be waiting with the hot chocolate and warm, dry clothes. Of course, when she'd see the frozen condition we were in, she'd always have to remark, "Why do you stay out so long?" Good question! The next day as we'd walk back out there, we'd both agree that as soon as we started to get cold, we'd head for home. But we never did. We were having too much fun.

One afternoon during Christmas vacation, Donna Walker stopped by with her mom for a visit. Donna was about seven years older than me. We weren't close friends, but because our families were, we would see each other from time to time. We had just come back from the ice pond and were thawing out. Donna said that sounded like fun. "Hey, can I come with you guys tomorrow? I have skates." Of course, we told her she could. The problem with Donna was that she was extremely heavy and we weren't sure how she would manage to skate. The following morning Donna arrived all ready and anxious to skate. By the time we walked to the pond, we could tell that she already seemed tired. We all laced up and started skating. And for a while we had fun. She wasn't a very good skater, but then neither were we. Most of the time was spent falling down and getting back up. We'd been there about an hour, and the temperature was rapidly dropping. We knew we wouldn't be able to stay out as long as usual. After another half hour or so, my feet were like ice. "Tommy, I'm going home. I'm freezing." "Okay, I'm cold, too." Donna said, "I'm going to skate one more time around." With that she took off, and while she was at the far end of the pond, away from us, she suddenly tripped and fell hard on the ice. "Why isn't she getting up?" I asked Tommy. He yelled out to her, "Hey, Donna, don't just lay on the ice. Get up, you're going to get even colder." She managed to holler out something but we couldn't hear her clearly. "We better go over there. I think something is wrong," he said. We both ran across the ice until we reached her. "I can't get up," she said. "You'll have to help me." Well, we tried to lift her but it was impossible. She was just too heavy. She kept complaining, too, that her leg hurt. We didn't know what to do. Tommy said, "Linda, you stay here with her and I'll run home and tell mom what happened." "No way," I said. "The last time you told me to stay put you went in the house and left me out in the tent. I'm going with you." "No, we can't just leave her here by herself. This isn't a joke, Linda. She's hurt and we can't pick her up. She'll freeze to death if she's out here much longer." "Fine, then I'll go for help and you can stay." "Linda, I can run much faster than you. Besides, I'm sure Donna would rather have you sit with her. I'll be back as soon as I can with help." I knew he was right. Donna couldn't be left alone, so I agreed to stay while he ran for help.

After what seemed like an eternity waiting for help to arrive, I was beginning to worry. "Tommy wouldn't be that mean and leave us out in the cold, would he?" I wondered. Finally, I could see in the distance several people walking toward the pond. When Tommy reached home and told mom what had happened, she immediately called Mr. Walker and told him about Donna's plight. He came over right away and the three of them walked out to the pond. When Mr. Walker tried to pick up Donna, she winced with pain. "I think her leg might be broken, or maybe badly sprained," he said. "In either case, even if I get her up, she can't walk. I'll be back with the pickup." Once again, there we sat, but mom did bring along several blankets to wrap around Donna to try and keep her warm, and a thermos of hot chocolate for us to share. A few minutes later when Mr. Walker returned, he, mom and Tommy picked Donna up and put her in the back of the truck and off we all went. The next day we found out that she had broken a small bone in her ankle and would be in a cast for a while. That was the end of her skating days.

As much as we loved winter, after many months of it, we welcomed a change. Grass turning green, leaves sprouting on the trees, tulips and daffodils popping out of the ground, the robin making its first appearance, and of course, the rebirth of dandelions — all signs that winter was finally behind us. Glorious spring had arrived, and that meant new things to fill our time. At the first hint of warm weather, I was out on the driveway making hopscotch squares, and Doris and I would play for hours.

Jump ropes and batons would also come out, again the two of us would play, until she was called home to work. Then I was on my own, but I didn't mind. Just to be outdoors and breathe the beautiful fresh air, especially after a rain, was heavenly. Our street didn't have sidewalks; instead there was a deep ditch. After a heavy rain the ditch would fill up, and on days warm enough, Tommy and I would go out to play in it. "We're only going to go wading, mom," we promised. We'd take our shoes and socks off, roll up our pants legs, and go splashing back and forth in the ditch. And before we'd know it, of course, we'd be soaked from head to toe. When mom would look out the window and see us, she'd immediately come out and yell that we were going to catch our "death of cold," whatever that really means. We always managed to convince her that since we were already wet, we might as well play for a little bit longer.

We also had a swing set that came to life in the spring. This wasn't the typical swing set that you can purchase today. This one was huge. Dad bought some pipe, dug four holes, cemented them into the ground, bought long chains, made two seats — best swing set in town. No matter what else we had planned for the day, we always found time to play on the swing set at least once a day. We loved it. One of our favorite things to do was to get as high as we could, then at the count of three, we'd jump off, seeing who could jump the farthest. I never won. Another contest we'd have would be to kick our shoes off, and again see whose shoe would go the farthest. This I could win (sometimes).

Mom loved Easter and she really got into it. Coloring eggs was always a big deal. She'd make three or four dozen eggs and Tommy and I would spend an entire night coloring them. Our Easter baskets were something to treasure. When we were quite young, she bought us each a large basket that would be used every year for as long as we got baskets. She'd fill them with an assortment of candies and we always got one huge chocolate cream egg that had our name on it. For me, my basket would always include a large jar of bubbles, plus various other outdoor things: jump rope, baton, jacks. Tommy always got a new model airplane and a few cars. He'd usually share the cars with me, always giving me the ones he liked least, naturally. Mom would wrap the baskets in bright colored cellophane and hide them. And boy, could she hide them. Some Easter mornings it would take us quite a while to find them, but the hunt was part of the fun. And though they didn't fit in the baskets, we always got a new kite. With all the vacant land around us, it was an ideal place for flying kites. We'd fly them for hours, and if one of ours ended up high in a tree, mom would take some old newspapers and make new ones for us. They weren't as pretty, but they still flew just as good.

For the past year Linda had been begging for a two-wheel bike. Tommy had gotten one the year before. This past Easter, after getting their Easter baskets, mom said she had a surprise

for Linda. They went outside and there in the driveway was a bike. Linda thought it was the most beautiful bike in the world. Mom had bought it at a second hand shop. It was in pretty bad condition, but after she got through with it, it almost looked like new. Mom had painted it a bright red and the handlebars had been painted silver. She had also bought a new seat and handle grips with streamers, and had added a nice basket. Every day after school and on weekends, Linda spent every spare moment riding that bike.

When school let out for the summer, their cousin, Kerry, came out to spend a month with them. Linda was so excited. The morning Kerry arrived, Linda had sat on the front porch swing anxiously waiting her arrival. Kerry didn't have a bike either, and Linda couldn't wait to show off the new bike to her.

"Mom, come quick, they're here." Mom, dad and Tommy come outside to greet them. Linda gave Kerry a big hug and said, "Wait till you see what I have." She directed Kerry's attention to the bike. "Wow, that's nice, Linda. Guess what…I got one too."

Just then, Linda watched as Uncle Larry took Kerry's new bike from the trunk of his car. A brand new Schwinn. It was the most beautiful new, shiny blue bike she had ever seen. Linda kept staring at the bike, then back at her own bike. She still loved her bike but it suddenly didn't look quite so pretty any more. And she wouldn't get a brand new one until Jerry Miller "borrowed" this one.

No matter what time of year, no matter what the weather, Tommy and I played. With a little imagination and determination, we could turn the simplest thing into hours of enjoyment. Sometimes it seems like a life time ago — other times it seems like only yesterday. As the years passed, we would enter our teenage years and then adulthood. There would be many new adventures and challenges awaiting us. But it is the memories of my childhood, growing up with Tommy, that warm my heart and make me smile. Mom loved being a homemaker and never seemed to tire of it. I can't ever remember her wishing she had time for herself, or needing to "get away" from it all for a while. Dad, easy going that he was, pretty much sat back and let mom run the house. It made for a happy childhood — one I'm so grateful for and will never forget.

2004 - Back to the Future

My 60th birthday came and went. My family surprised me by taking me downtown to Chicago to see a play, "Tony and Tina's Wedding." Dinner was served during the play, and afterwards we all went across the street to a bar for drinks and a night of lively conversation. It was a lovely way to celebrate my 60th birthday. My daughter made me a memory book filled with wonderful photos and stories. It was the highlight of the night. And as we all looked through the scrapbook, much of the night was spent saying to someone, "Do you remember...?" and then we'd all start sharing stories. It's what I love to do. Remember the past. But equally, I embrace the present, and look forward to the future.

Sadly, many people are no longer with me. My beloved father had a stroke in 1971 at the age of 57. It left his right side paralyzed and confined to a wheel chair. It was heartbreaking.

Three years later he had another stroke and passed away in 1974, three days after his 60th birthday. Far too young to die, it left me devastated. He's been gone 30 years now, but at times, I still feel his presence, especially when I've spent the day with Uncle Charley, or when I sit down at the piano. To this day, I still play some of the songs he taught me, and it always brings a smile to my face. How fortunate I was to have a dad like him. I loved him so, and he will live on forever in my heart.

My wonderful mom is also gone. In 1983 she was diagnosed with Alzheimer's disease. The disease ravaged on for nearly 13 years until she passed away in 1995 at the age of 75. The cruelty of the disease is indescribable, unless you've lived through a loved one afflicted with it. I miss her so much. I don't think there is a day that goes by that I don't think about her. A few years ago I saw a movie called "Peggy Sue Got Married," about a woman who goes back in time and spends a few days with her family as a young girl. I remember crying as I watched it and thinking how wonderful it would be if I could spend just one more day with her. One more time to run in the house after a long day of play and have her waiting there. One more time to get tucked into bed by her. At a recent class reunion last year, I was touched by how many people came up to me and immediately inquired about mom, and then they would go on and on remembering when she worked at Willies, and how much they liked her. She was truly the most unselfish woman I ever knew, always putting her family first. I loved her so, and like dad, she lives on forever in my heart.

Mom was a homemaker. It's what she loved to do, and it showed in everything she did. The following poem (by Helen Steiner Rice) was read at her funeral service. It is such a beautiful poem, and though it wasn't written for her, it couldn't be more fitting.

MOTHER'S DON'T DIE

When we are children, we are happy and gay
And our mother is young and she laughs as we play,
Then as we grow up, she teaches us truth
And lays life's foundation in the days of our youth—
And then it is time for us to leave home
But her teachings go with us wherever we roam,
For all that she taught us and all that she did
when we were just a little kid.
We will often remember and then realize
That mothers are special and wonderfully wise...
And as she grows older, we look back with love,
Knowing that mothers are *"Gifts from above,"*
And when she "goes home" to receive her reward,
She will dwell in God's Kingdom and "keep house for the Lord"
Where she'll light up the stars that shine through the night,
And keep all the moonbeams sparkling and bright.

Hamlin Avenue

  And then with the dawn she'll put the darkness away
  As she scours the sun to new brilliance each day...
  So dry tears of sorrow, for mothers don't die—
  They just move in with God and "keep house in the sky,"
  And there in God's Kingdom, mothers watch from above
  Looking after their children with undying love!

  Tommy, who to this day continues to make me laugh, lives in New Kensington, Pennsylvania, just outside of Pittsburgh, with his wife, the former Francine Bartolacci, and their daughter, Elizabeth, age 11, (named after our mom). He and Francine own a printing and publishing business. Their daughter fills their world with joy. He was previously married to MaryAnne Hamilton, and has two kids from that marriage, Lisa and Christopher. They are great kids and are doing well. They both reside in the Chicago area where they own two restaurants called Costello Sandwich & Sides. Excellent food!! Lisa and her husband, Jake Crampton, have two young sons, Donald, (DC), and Charley. Chris recently married a lovely young lady, Kathy Richardson.

  The house on Hamlin Avenue is no longer there. In 1963, with me married and out of the house, and Tommy away at college, mom and dad thought the house was too big for just the two of them. They sold it to a family with young kids, and built a much smaller home on the vacant lot next to it. When I'd be at mom's visiting, I'd see the new kids in the yard playing, and wonder if they were enjoying the big, old house as much as Tommy and I did, if they were making wonderful memories as we did. About 10 years later, Doris called to tell me that the house had been destroyed by fire. Hearing that news broke my heart. That wonderful house... gone forever. No more laughter would be heard from within its walls. The little street I grew up on would never be the same. The old saying, "you can't go home again," came to mind. Sad, but true.

Last year I went back to Markham. In addition to driving around the town, past the houses where Barb, Judy, and Sue used to live, past the schools we attended, I drove down Hamlin Avenue. It had been many years since I had been there. In some ways I'm sorry I went back, because it was barely recognizable as the street where I grew up, where Tommy and I had so much fun, and made wonderful memories. Where our house used to be, stands a new brick home. The yard we played in looks completely different, and with the side lot no longer empty, it looks much smaller, too. Gone is the ditch in front where we used to go wading. The giant tree Tommy and I used to climb is gone. The vacant field behind the house where Tommy and I built our roads and villages in the ditch, and further out where we used to ice skate, is now replaced by more homes. All of our neighbors, the Willmer's, Brandy's, and Walker's, have passed away and their homes are also gone, all replaced by large new ones. It was a sad day for me. Thank God for memories.

Hamlin Avenue

After leaving Hamlin Avenue, I needed something to cheer me up, and I knew exactly what would do the trick. I drove the few blocks to Willies WeeNee Wagon for a hot dog. Willie passed away about five years ago, and the business is now owned by his son. The original wagon has been replaced, but once inside, I could still feel mom's presence everywhere. I could picture her working behind the counter, running the place to perfection. And as a further reminder, photographs of her taken by Willie many years ago, grace the walls of the Wagon. When I finished eating, I left with a smile on my face.

My Aunt Honey was a big part of my life growing up, and she still is today. She lives fairly close to me so about once a month I take her out to breakfast where we catch up on the latest family stuff. Her husband, George, passed away a number of years ago. She has one son, also George, who is one of the kindest and nicest persons I know.

My Grandma Mary passed away nearly 20 years ago and I still think of her often, especially the years she lived with us. A field of bright yellow dandelions in early spring brings a smile to my face. I always think of her with her shopping bag in tow, picking them for our supper.

My cousin, Kerry Edelman Gore, still lives in the Chicago area with her husband Al. They have four kids, Kevin, Brian, Kim and Alan, Jr. She is blessed with five grandchildren. Her mom, my Aunt Dee, passed away two years ago. We all mourned her death. She was a kind and caring person. Kerry and her

2004- BACK TO THE FUTURE

husband also own a home on Redstone Lake in Wisconsin. In the summer, my husband, Bob, and I go up there with our grandkids for a long weekend. Kerry's kids and grandkids also come up and we have a wonderful time. It takes me back to when we were all kids and the summer's we spent at Honey Lake.

My cousin, Jan Morsi Sellards, also lives in the Chicago area. She recently retired after a long and successful career in telemarketing. Her father, George, passed away 10 years ago, and her mom, my Aunt Di, lives with her. I don't see Aunt Di as much as I'd like but I do talk to her on the phone a lot, where we'll chat endlessly about everything and anything. She's getting up in years but still as feisty and amusing as ever. I get together several times a year with Kerry and Jan for dinner…just the three of us, and it's like old times when we were kids. I love them dearly.

In the summer of 2001, Kerry, Jan and I (along with Aunt Di, Kerry's daughter, Kim, and my husband, Bob) drove up to Honey Lake. It had been 45 years since I was there, but the wonderful memories are as clear as ever. Just the sound of "Honey Lake" evokes warm and fuzzy feelings. They suggest a moment when time stood still and everything was beautiful, and the world smelled so good and we would be young forever. The trip was everything I had hoped it would be. The cottage itself is no longer there but we were able to stand on the location where it once was and take some pictures. Although the town changed a lot, we could still visualize how it used to be. The big hill we used to climb many times each day remains, but rather than gravel, it is now paved. When we approached the hill, we stopped the car and decided the three of us, for old times sake, would walk up to the top. About half way up the hill, I realized I was huffing and puffing and thinking to myself, "How did we do this over and over with no problem." I thought I was the only one thinking that, when suddenly both Kerry and Jan let out a loud "Whoo" and commented that they too were tired, and we were only half way up. Laughing, we trudged upward, making it to the top, but I can assure you, we didn't attempt to climb it more than once. The lake, itself, looked better than ever. The area was clean and the seaweed was gone. As we stood looking out at the water glistening in the sun, I could hear the sounds of our laughter so many summers ago, could picture our running and jumping in the water without a care in the world. It was a very special and nostalgic moment, almost the perfect day. The only thing missing for me was Tommy. If he had been there, it would have been the perfect day. Honey Lake will always have a special place in my heart.

As for my dad's family, of the eight kids, only my Uncle Charley and Aunt Ada are still here. I try to see Uncle Charley once or twice a year. He's a wonderful man, so much like my dad, not only in looks but so many of his mannerisms are the same. He recently lost his wife, Helen. She was a lovely lady and I know he misses her dearly. He has two grown children, Bill and Barbara.

Aunt Ada lives quite far from me so unfortunately I don't see her very often. She's a dear lady and I must mention that a lot of the pictures in this book were given to me by Aunt Ada. Some of the pictures of my dad as a young boy I had never seen before. Her husband, Sam, passed away in 1989. She has one daughter, Charlene, and one granddaughter, Samantha.

Recently I found out that Isabella, the aunt who remained in Italy, and whom none of us ever knew, has a grandson, Michael. Michael came to this country several years ago. He was able to locate some of our family, and for a while worked at my cousin Arthur's store. It's a small world.

As for my friends, after high school, I lost contact with them, but I'm happy to say all that has changed now.

Two years ago I got an e-mail from Sue Donnelly Stolz letting me know her mom had passed away. I was very sad to receive that news. Her mother was very special to me. I went to the wake, and though I'm sorry it wasn't under better circumstances, it did get Sue and me back together again. And it's been simply wonderful. We now see each other a few times a year and e-mail all the time. Her mom lived in the same house Sue grew up in until the day she died. One day Sue called and said the house had been sold. She asked if I'd like to see it one last time. Did I ever. I met her at the house and I can't tell you the flood of memories it brought back. I had spent so much of my youth in that home…talking, dancing, dreaming, doing silly things…all the things young girls do. It was like coming home. Afterwards, we went out and had a very long lunch. It was a great day. Sue and I share the month of October for our birthdays. When we both turned 60, we went out to dinner to celebrate and had a wonderful time. She is such a special friend and to show her what she means to me, I wrote a poem which I gave to her that night at dinner. I also made a cassette tape for her featuring about 20 songs she and I used to love. True Oldies but Goodies! She, in return, presented me with a picture of the two of us taken in first grade, along with a current picture of the two of us. The caption reads, "From 6 to 60." It sits proudly on my desk where I can see it every day....a reminder of how grateful I am she is once again a part of my life. She's one of the kindest people I've ever known. Sue still lives in the Chicagoland area. She has two boys and is the proud grandmother of two.

Donna Olson Bondi is as beautiful today (inside and out) as she was 40 some years ago. Shortly after reconnecting with Sue, she called me one day and asked if I'd like to have dinner with Donna and her. I could hardly wait. I hadn't seen Donna in over 20 years. What a night we had. It was wonderful seeing her again. We seemed to connect in so many ways, and we've become even better friends today than ever. I treasure her friendship more than words can say. She also lives in the Chicagoland area, has two daughters and five grandkids who light up her life.

Barbara Lugar Barbre recently moved to Florida with her husband Bill. She has two kids and three beautiful granddaughters. As kids, Barb was one of my dearest friends. I regret deeply that the close friendship we once had is not what it used to be, but the wonderful memories of her and the good times we shared will always be one of the highlights of my youth.

Judy Porter Brandhorst is a terrific person — then and now. I hadn't seen Judy in over 20 years, but recently we reunited at a class reunion. It was so good to see her again. A few weeks after the reunion, we had dinner together and it was nice to spend time with her and catch up on everything that had happened over the years. She looks great and I feel so fortunate to have gotten reacquainted with her. She lives in the Chicagoland area with her husband David, has three kids and six grandchildren, including a set of twins born this past year. Life is grand!!

I hadn't seen Doris in almost 35 years. We'd talk on the phone every now and then, always saying that we'd get together, but somehow we never did. Recently, we got together and it was so emotional. We hugged, and got teary-eyed, and just had the best time reminiscing. When I left, after taking a few pictures, we vowed that we'd get together from time to time. And I plan to do just that. She still lives in Markham with her husband, Jimmy, has five kids, 14 grandkids, and two great grandkids, plus another on the way.

As for my life, it's been great. There were a few bumps along the way, but then whose life doesn't have a few. After high school, I worked for a short time, then married, as many girls did way back then, mainly because I think we didn't realize we had other choices. It just seemed the natural thing to do. I married a man named Steve Krause. He's a good man, but probably because we did marry so young, as the years went by and we both grew up, we wanted different things in life. The marriage ended after 18 years, but it did produce three wonderful kids. They are what gives my life meaning.

My daughter, Laurie, now 42, has always been, and always will be my best friend. There's probably no one I'm more comfortable with or whom I just enjoy being with. She's such a special person. She's married to a great guy, Laurens Van Luyk, whom she met in California when she was working out there. Thankfully, they returned to Chicago to get married and make their home here. She works for a software technology company.

Helping Laurie plan her wedding was a wonderful thing we shared. She planned to leave California and move back here several months ahead of Laurens so she could get settled and finalize the wedding plans. Rather than have her make the long drive back alone, as she planned to do, I flew out to California and then drove home with her. We took the southern route home, taking our slow, sweet time, and I must say, it was one of the most pleasurable trips I've ever taken. We talked and laughed, sang our heads off, played silly games and just had a great time together — just the two of us. I'm so thankful we shared that time, because I knew we would probably never have another opportunity like that again. Once we got home, we were busy with wedding preparations, and after her wedding, she would begin a new chapter in her life.

They have two boys who are the loves of my life. Thomas (named after my dad) is 12 years old and Joe is seven. Thomas is the more serious of the two. He's extremely bright and does very well in school. He loves sports, both playing and watching. Joe is very outgoing, also does well in school, and amuses everyone with his good-natured ways. They both make me laugh all the time. They are both so special in my life and I thank God for them every day.

My son, Steve, 41 years old, is simply put, a great person. As a young boy, he was always the thoughtful one, willing to give a hand to anyone. That has not changed over the years. He's a hard and dedicated worker and an all-around good person. He works for a large contracting firm, and is co-owner of a smaller construction company. He is married to the former Arness Goetz. I have a great relationship with her which I am so grateful for.

Steve and Arness have three kids who are equally the loves of my life. Stephen, 14, is such a cool kid. He makes me laugh all the time with some of the things he says and does. Kathryn, nine, is my little angel, just as cute as can be. She loves to draw — maybe she'll be an artist some day. She seems to have a talent for it. Lauren Newquist, 18, is a beautiful and special young lady. I met Lauren when she was just over three years old, and fell in love with her instantly. She graduated high school this year and started college this fall. Where did the years go? They're all wonderful kids, and along with Thomas and Joe, they bring such joy to my life.

Tim, now 40, is "my baby." As a child he was always the adventurous one, and that has carried on into adulthood. His passions are traveling and fishing. He's an excellent musician, playing drums, and for many years he played in a band, actually several bands, but one in particular, Gringo, was wonderful. We spent many Saturday nights going downtown to hear them play. It was a fun time in all our lives. He was married briefly to a lovely young lady he met while vacationing in Italy. Tim is now living in Alaska where he manages an auto body shop. When not working, he does what he loves best — fly fishing. I was heartbroken when he moved so far away, but he's living the life he wants, and I wouldn't have it any other way.

For the past 23 years, I have been married to Bob Maurer, and I thank God every day for him. He's a great guy. Now retired, Bob worked 32+ years in telecommunications. We enjoy a lot of the same things and it's been a good marriage. He's been very good to my kids over the years, for which I'm grateful, and he absolutely adores my grandkids. They all call him "Grandpa" and enjoy being with him. He spends a lot of time with them playing monopoly, checkers, and chess, or just horsing around. He taught them how to play poker last year. They get a big kick out of that. The last few years we've been taking them on vacation and have the time of our life with them.

Bob was also married once before and he has a son, Tony (42) and a daughter, Diana (39), from that marriage. Tony is married to Fran Armstrong and they have three beautiful girls:

Grace (11), Lydia (9), and Natalie (4). Unfortunately, we live quite some distance from them so we don't see them as often as we would like. Tony is co-owner of a successful computer software firm, and when he isn't working or spending time with his family, he enjoys spending his time on Lake Michigan in his 30 ft. sailboat.

Diana is currently single. She's a bright girl but in recent years has had some personal struggles to deal with. We all love and care about her, and hope that she will find a way to get her life back together. Recently, she has been doing just that, and we're all so proud of her. In the meantime, thankfully, she and I get along very well. We share a passion for figure skating and have a fun time together watching skating on TV.

Although this book is all about my youth, I need to mention one person. Though she wasn't part of my childhood, she became a very important part of my adult life. For many years, my life revolved around raising my kids. I was so busy, it didn't occur to me how much I missed having close friends. Once the kids were all in school, with each passing year, I found myself with more time on my hands and began to really regret that I had lost touch with all my old friends. Then I met Pat Mango and she has been my closest friend for the past 35 years. Together, we've had the time of our life. Talking, traveling, shopping, laughing, crying — we've done it all. We've been there for each other through good times and difficult times. She's a special person and I'm blessed to have her friendship. She and her husband, Vince, have three daughters and seven grandkids. Tragedy struck her family two years ago. Pat's beautiful granddaughter, Kelly (9), died suddenly. The pain and sorrow she and her family went through is unfathomable, and to see my friend go through this was agonizing. They're a close and loving family, and that love and closeness has given them the strength to go on. Pat's daughter, Bobbi (Kelly's mom), is one of the most loving, caring, and courageous people I've ever known. If I were to make a list of people I admire most, Bobbi would be right up near the top. She's an amazing woman, and I care so much for her. When something like this happens, it makes you even more aware of just how fragile life is, and how important it is to not only embrace each day that is given to us, but to embrace the family and friends who make each day special.

Three other women have enriched my life. Jeanette Millar, Barbara Shymkovich, and Barb Gabriel all were an important part of my life at various times.

I met Jeanette Millar when I was expecting my second child. She lived across the street from me and was pregnant with her fourth child. We had a lot in common and became good friends, Two years later she moved to Colorado, and for a number of summers, until the kids reached school age, I would travel by train with my three kids and visit her. Those were fun times. I didn't see her for at least 15 years, but several years ago she and her husband were in the Chicago area and we got to spend a day together. It was like old times, minus seven kids running around.

2004- BACK TO THE FUTURE

Barbara Shymkovich and I worked together for five years, and a better co-worker one couldn't have. She made going to work fun. We became good friends and had many fun times together. She moved to California about 20 years ago and regrettably, I haven't seen her since. We send each other a Christmas card each year along with a nice letter filling each other in on what is going on in our lives. And as nice as that is, it would be twice as nice to actually spend some time with her again.

In the early 1980's, I worked for an engineering consulting firm. Barb Gabriel was one of the engineering consultants I worked for. Without a doubt, she's the smartest woman I have ever known...also one of the funniest. She has the most delightful sense of humor and made me laugh all the time. We had great times together, and I consider it an honor to be her friend. A bit of irony here... while I was working for her, she wrote a book. Being her secretary, I typed it for her. It was a technical book on scanning electron microscopy (told you she was smart)! So now I can tell her I wrote a book, too, albeit far from the intellectual quality of hers. She lives in Virginia and it has been at least 10 years, maybe longer, since I've seen her. And if I'm ever fortunate enough to see her again, within minutes she'll have me laughing my head off.

I'm grateful for all three of their friendships and the good times we shared.

As I reflect on my life, I realize how blessed I've been. It's been a wonderful life and I wouldn't trade it for the world. My parents provided a loving home for Tommy and me. We were their life and it showed in everything they did. I miss them dearly every day of my life. Tommy continues to be my idol. He still makes me laugh all the time, and I can't imagine a life without him. I've been blessed with three wonderful kids who in turn blessed me with kind and loving grandkids. They truly fill my life with joy. My extended family continues to be an important part of my life. I have friends that I cherish and every moment with them is special. Finally, a husband who is good and caring, and makes growing older fun.

Life has been good to me. I'm thankful for everyone who has touched my life.

New Kensington, Pennsylvania - July 17, 2004

Linda is visiting Tommy. She drove out here with her daughter, Laurie, and four grandkids for a brief vacation. The weather has been cool and rainy. Not like mid-July should be. Nevertheless, they've been having lots of fun. Today was spent sightseeing in downtown Pittsburgh, dodging raindrops. After a rather late dinner, everyone is exhausted and have all turned in for the night. All except Tommy and Linda. They are in his den enjoying a nightcap.

"Hey, Linda, remember all the fun we used to have at Riverview?"

"*Of course, I do. It was the greatest amusement park in the world. We had so much fun.*"

"*Well, tomorrow we're all going to Kennywood for the day. The rain should be out of the area and it's supposed to warm up. It should be a beautiful day. They have some really great rollercoasters. We'll have so much fun — just like when we were kids. How does that sound?*"

"*Sounds like lots of fun. I can hardly wait. I've told the grandkids many times about the fun we used to have at Riverview when we were kids. But I'm telling you right now, I am not going on any rides that look scary. I remember all too well how you'd talk me into going on rides always telling me how much fun we'd have. Silly me, I'd believe you. Then we'd get on the rides and I'd be scared out of my wits while you sat there laughing.*"

"*Oh, come on, Linda, that was a long time ago. I just liked to tease you. We're all grown up now. You don't have to go on any rides you don't like. We'll have a great time with all the kids.*"

Kennywood Park, July 18, 2004

After several cool, rainy days, today is beautiful. The sun is shining and just a few lofty clouds fill the sky. Picture perfect! The grandkids and Elizabeth are having a ball, running from one ride to the next, with several stops in between for cotton candy, popcorn and ice cream. It's almost 1:00 and despite the snacking, we're hungry.

"*Linda,*" *Francine says,* "*as soon as the kids get off this ride,* lets get some lunch." "Sounds good to me. I'm starving. Running around this park works up an appetite."

After we've all placed our order, pizza for the kids (naturally), Italian sausage sandwiches for Tommy and Linda, and some kind of stir fry for Francine and Laurie, they sit down to enjoy the lunch, chattering nonstop about all the rides they've been on, and what's next to go on.

When lunch is finished, Tommy says, "Hey Linda, let's go on Jack Rabbit."

"Not a chance. That's not for me. It looks too scary. Take the kids. Laurie will go, too. I'll wait with Francine."

"Aw, come on, Linda. Look at it...it's a fun rollercoaster, just lots of gentle ups and downs. It's not a scary ride. Please, come on with me?"

"I don't know. It looks too steep. Are you sure I'm not going to fly out of my seat like I did on the Bobs years ago? You know I hate that."

"Absolutely not. It's a smooth ride."

"Promise?"

"Cross my heart. Would I kid you? You'll love it."

Although somewhat hesitant, I agree and we get in line. Tommy gets in the car first with Stephen. "Hey, Linda, sit right behind me with Thomas."

"Okay, but I thought we were going to ride together."

"Oh well, I'm seated now. Maybe later we'll sit together on another ride."

Settled into the seat behind him with Thomas, the ride begins. The slow climb up the first hill seems like forever. Finally, just as we reach the top of the hill, Tommy turns around and yells, "Have fun, Linda." The last thing she sees as she goes plummeting down the steep slope, flying half way out of her seat, is the big smile on Tommy's face. The only thing louder than his roaring laughter is the blood curdling scream coming from Linda. It was going to be a very long ride.

Sixty-two years old and some things never change. Where Tommy is concerned, the adage "Older but wiser" definitely does not apply to Linda.

Tom & Linda in 2003 at Chris & Kathy's wedding

My husband, Bob and I (1994)

Bob and I outside on our deck in August, 2002

Tom, Francine and Elizabeth

Tom and his daughter, Elizabeth with Toms's grandson, DC (2003)

My daughter Laurie & I (1990)

My son Steve and I (2004)

Me with my son Tim on his 40th birthday. The next day he would move to Alaska. July 25, 2004.

Tim fishing in Alaska - 2004

Laurie, her husband Laurens (1997)

Steve & his wife, Arness (2004)

Tom's Daughter Lisa, her husband Jake, and son DC (2003)

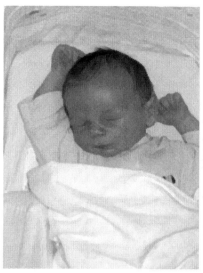

Lisa and Jake's Newest born son, Charlie (2004)

Tom's son Chris with his new bride, Kathy (2003)

*My grandkids in 1999:
Thomas, Stephen, Lauren, Joe & Kathryn*

*My grandkids: Thomas, Joe, Lauren, Kathryn & Stephen (2004)
Thomas & Joe are my daughter Laurie's boys.
Lauren, Stephen & Kathryn are my son Steve's kids*

Jan, Linda & Kerry (2002)

*Our trip back to Honey Lake 2002
Kerry, Linda & Jan*

*Jan, Linda & Kerry
On the bridge at Honey Lake 2002*

*1989 - Aunt Honey, Aunt Di, Mom, Aunt Dee. This would be the final time
mom would see her sisters all together again.*

Aunt Honey with her son George (2002)

Linda with Uncle Charley (2003)   *My kids father, Steve Krause (1961)*

Aunt Mary's 80th birthday party: Aunt Ada, Uncle Frank, Aunt Mary, Aunt Donna, Mom, Uncle Charley

Lisa and Chris with their mom, Mary Anne (late 1980's)

Bob and I at his son Tony and Fran's wedding (1989)

Bob's granddaughters: Lydia, Natalie & Grace (2003)

Bob's daughter, Diana (1992)

Pat Mango, Bob & Me at our wedding in 1981

*Kelly Hanlon
In Loving Memory
1992-2002*

Linda and Pat (2002)

Dinner with my dear friends: Sue Donnelly Stolz, Linda, & Donna Olson Bondi (2003)

Linda with Barbara Lugar Barbre (2004)

Judy Porter Brandhorst (2003)

Linda and Jeanette Millar in 2002 on their visit back to Chicago

Linda and Barbara Shymkovich in 1982 at an office Halloween party

Linda with childhood neighbor, Doris Willmer (2004)

*Kennywood Park 2004 standing in front of the Thunderbolt
Stephen, Joe, Tom, Thomas & Linda*

*Here we are at Seven Springs ski resort outside Pittsburgh (2004)
From left: Francine, Stephen, Tom, Thomas, Elizabeth, Linda,
Kathryn, Laurie & Joe*

*At Costello Sandwich & Sides (Lisa & Chris's restaurant) 2002
From left: Jan, Lisa, Aunt Di, Kerry, Kim, Linda, Bob & Jake*

Tom, Francine, Lisa, Elizabeth and Chris in Chicago (1999)

POEMS BY LINDA COSTELLO MAURER

TURNING 60

I look in the mirror and what do I see…
An aging woman, is this really me?
My minds drifts back to another day,
When I was just a young girl at play.

I miss my mom and I miss my dad,
and I miss the childhood that I had.
I miss being young, feeling safe and secure,
When the world seemed much more wholesome and pure.

I miss my brother, he's my link with the past.
I wish he lived closer, time's going by fast.
I love him dearly, he makes me smile,
If we could be kids again, just for a while.

But time marches on, a new decade I near,
And I reflect on those that I hold dear.

At the top of the list of my life story,
Of course would be Steve, Tim, and Laurie.

The three of them are my heart's delight
They make a cloudy day sunny and bright.
I love them more than words can say,
And pray God keep them safe each day.

And now I'm blessed even more than before,
I have grandkids whom I simply adore.
Stephen's so special, he outshines the rest,
And precious Thomas, he's simply the best.

Kathryn's my angel, so pretty and smart,
And Joe, from day one, he captured my heart.
And beautiful Lauren, she's such a delight,
From the moment I met her, it was love at first sight.

I'm thankful Bob is a part of my life,
I love him and I'm glad I'm his wife.
Family and friends make life worth living,
Every day with them is truly Thanksgiving.

So as I turn 60, I can truly say,
I've had a good life and I cherish each day.
I look forward to the future, I embrace the past,
Life is a blessing; long may it last.

October 2002

Friendship Remembered

I remember a young Sue & Linda,
As friends we go back a long way...
It's hard to believe these same two girls
Are celebrating "60" today!

I remember with fondness your mom and your dad,
And Donnie, Teri and Dru;
But the things that I remember the most,
Are the good times I shared with you.

I remember the house you grew up in,
We'd dance on your living room rug,
And listening to our favorite records,
We perfected our "jitterbug."

I remember we'd talk on the phone every night,
About boys and "what to wear."
We'd discuss the latest gossip, of course,
Always offering our own fair share!

I remember we laughed at "an unicorn,"
The banana boat sounded divine;
But the thing we laughed the hardest at,
Was a line from the song "Clementine"!

Hamlin Avenue

I remember Friday night square dancing,
We always had so much fun.
We'd "doh-si-doh" to "Oh, Johnny, Oh"
Our "foursome" was Number One!

I remember our years at Bremen
Some of it bittersweet-
At pow-wows we would dance and stroll
Till we could hardly stand on our feet.

I remember tobogganing and Captain Jinks,
And playing Kick the Can,
Going downtown to Ho Sei Gai
And being an Elvis fan.

I remember the singing group we had,
I think we were called Teen Toppers,
It was lots of fun, but I'm sure you'd agree
We would never have become "show stoppers"!

Many years have passed since that time of our youth,
But one thing I know to be true..
I'll always remember with love and affection,
A special friend named Sue.

Written for Sue Donnelly on the occasion of our 60th birthdays
(October 2002)

ODE TO LAURENS

We're all so excited, in fact you might say
We're simply bursting with joy.
And all because you're coming here
To live in Illinois.

The summers here are hot and sticky,
In the autumn leaves will fall.
Springtime brings the wind and rain,
Boy, we've got it all.

Chicago winters aren't really that bad,
In fact, they're kind of nice....
That is, if you can overlook
The cold, the snow, the ice.

We don't have mountains, an ocean or palm trees,
and you won't get a year round tan -
But there's something much more exciting here,
You can be a CHICAGO BEARS FAN!!

In no time at all, you'll feel right at home,
You'll take the weather in stride.
And when its 20 below with 3 feet of snow,

You'll think, "I did this all for my bride?"

All in all, it will be quite a change
Don't want it to get you down,
So we're sending you a few little things,
To help you prepare for our town.

Can't wait for you two to get here,
We're really in our glory.
Have a very Merry Christmas,
All my love to you and Laurie.

Written for my future son-in-law the Christmas before he and my daughter were married (December 1989)

To My Daughter

It seems like only yesterday,
My head was in a whirl.
When the doctor smiled at me and said,
"You've got a little girl!"

And such a sheer delight it was,
To watch you grow and grow.
Romping in the summer sun,
Or playing in the snow.

I still recall so vividly
Your playing on the swing.
And in the house your father'd say,
"Just listen to Streisand sing"!

From toddler to teenager,
The years went by so fast.
Now you're a young lady
With only memories of the past.

The day you left to move out west,
I thought my heart would break.
It seemed like such a big thing
For you to undertake.

But now you're coming home to us,
You're about to become a bride.
You'll be standing at the altar
With Laurens by your side.

I'll watch so very lovingly
As you become his wife.
But in my heart you'll always be
My little girl for life.

I thank the Good Lord every day,
Who looks down from up above.
For sending me a little girl
To fill my world with love.

Written for my daughter Laurie, given to her at her bridal shower (May 1990)

40 Years Of Laurie

On this your 40th birthday,
I thought I'd take some time.
To stroll down memory lane with you,
and put it all in rhyme.

Growing up with Steve and Tim,
They were your two best friends.
They teased you and bugged you, but mostly they loved you,
Except when you tattled on them.

Barbie dolls with Colleen and Jackie,
and, of course, with Brenda, too.
Riding bikes, or flying kites,
Always something exciting to do.

Rosie, Traveller, Ginger and Poke,
Spooky, Dixie and Zack (what a joke)!
Mitzi, Pepper, Kitty and Max,
Romeo, Ollie, no time to relax.
Can't forget Clancy, Twiggy and Beau,
Enough pets? I think so!

Hamlin Avenue

Grandma Costello, now you were her pet.
How she loved to spoil you.
You sure kept her hopping, with everyday shopping
and you always got something brand new.

Bell bottoms, hip huggers, mood rings were in,
Shoes were your biggest delight.
You loved scary ghost stories, and fresh morning glories,
and singing Queen Bee late at night.

When it came to being daring and bold,
You were heads above the rest.
You're funny and witty, you'll sing any ditty,
You are the absolute best.

You smelled clean with Lifebuoy,
Cured a headache with Bayer,
Caused hyperventilation one day—
When the super bowl shuffle caused feathers to ruffle,
They've no humor up in Green Bay.

My favorite story was down in Missouri,
When the window just wouldn't come down.
We lay there in bed as rain poured on our head,
We're lucky that we didn't drown.

I hope you enjoyed this brief look in time,

Now its back to the future for you.

May your life be aglow, with Tom, Laurens and Joe,

And may all of your wishes come true.

Written for Laurie's 40 birthday (April 2002)

To My Son, Steve

It seems like only yesterday,
My world was filled with joy.
When the doctor smiled at me and said,
"You've got a little boy"!!

Watching you grow up each day,
Filled my heart with awe.
For you simply were the cutest little boy
I'd ever saw.

From early on your kindness showed,
In everything you did,
Your generous and loving ways
Made you a special kid.

Growing up the middle child
Wasn't always an easy task.
You were always there for Laurie & Tim ,
No matter what they'd ask.

You always made our family proud,
Of this I can avow.
Your grandparents loved you dearly,
How I wish they could see you now.

Riding horses on Dead Dog Road,
Going to horse shows, too.
Spending a summer on Lloyd Terry's farm,
There was always something to do.

Building a two-story treehouse,
Catching Romeo just for a lark,
Going to Shores of Killarney,
Playing out late after dark.

Being raised a "country" boy,
Was hard work but lots of fun,
Repairing fences or cleaning the stalls,
There was always some work to be done.

We teased you about your "Licorice Stick,"
As you'd practice every day.
But my heart would swell, & I'd burst with pride,
When I'd listen to you play.

I remember the day you joined the Marines,
My heart, it broke in two.
I didn't want you leaving,
I knew I would worry about you.

But once again you made me proud,
With flying colors you came through,
When you set your mind to something
There's nothing you can't do.

The years have passed so quickly,
You're no longer a little boy,
You've got your own great family now,
To fill our lives with joy.

I love you more than words can say,
May God look after you.
May he keep you safe and happy,
In every thing you do.

So Happy 40th Birthday, Steve-
You know I'm your Number One fan.
My special little boy is now
A very special Man.

Written for Steve's 40th birthday (June 2003)

To My Son, Tim

On the glorious day that you were born
I knew right from the start,
You were someone very special
And I loved you with all my heart.

From early on you made me smile,
With everything you did.
Your temper would flare, but then in a flash,
You'd be a loving kid.

When you'd get mad those chubby cheeks
Looked like they would explode.
You'd huff and puff, and look so cute...
Your dad nicknamed you Toad.

You were always up at the crack of dawn,
Ready for some new thrill.
You tackled everything with zest
You never could sit still.

Growing up with Laurie and Steve,
You worked hard and had fun at play.
Your grandparents loved you dearly,
How I wish they could see you today.

Hamlin Avenue

On a skateboard you were awesome,
Your punching bag sure took a pounding.
And the way you worked those numchucks...
Well, it truly was astounding.

When it came to riding horses,
You were heads above the rest.
Racing around the barrels,
You and Rosie were the best.

Going to watch you play in bands
Are nights I'll never forget...
Gringo, to me, is still the very
Best band I've seen yet.

Wanderlust is in your blood
You have a need to roam.
You can travel the world all over
As long as you come back home.

The day you moved to Italy,
Was more than I could bear.
Selfishly I wanted you here
Instead of over there.

Now once again you're about to move
To a place so far away,
And once again I pray
That you'll come back home some day.

The little boy I loved so much
And gave me so much joy,
Is all grown up but in my heart,
Remains my little boy.

So Happy 40th birthday, Tim,
I'm so very proud of you…
May you have good health and happiness
In everything you do.

May God send a Guardian Angel
To watch over you from above,
Whatever path in life you choose,
You'll always have my love.

Written for Tim's 40th birthday (July 2004)

FAMILY

For those who came before us
we salute you loud and clear.
We hold your memory close to us,
you always will be near.

The family tree keeps growing,
new generations come along.
They may march to a different drummer,
but they sing the same old song.

A song of peace for all on earth,
for a family strong and true.
A guiding light to help us
when we don't know what to do.

The eternal flame burns brightly,
it never will go out.
So hail the mighty family,
That's what life is all about.

Written for my Aunt Dee's memorial service (February 2002)

Remembering Kelly

You're the brightest star in the evening sky,
You're the tear that gently falls from my eye.
You're the warmth of the sun making everything bright,
You're the moonbeams that sparkle and shine late at night.

You're the cardinal I see at dawn's early light,
As it soars to the heavens in glorious flight.
You're the breath of fresh air that I breathe every day,
You're the fireflies nightly that come out to play.

You're the first one I think of each day as I rise,
And the last one at night as I close my eyes.
And though I can't hold you, we're never apart.
You live on forever in the depths of my heart.

In loving memory of Kelly Hanlon (1992-2002)